WITHDRAWN

HARVARD LIBRARY

WITHDRAWN

Henry Roe Cloud

A Biography

David W. Messer

Hamilton Books
A member of
The Rowman & Littlefield Publishing Group
Lanham • Boulder • New York • Toronto • Plymouth, UK

Copyright © 2010 by
Hamilton Books
4501 Forbes Boulevard
Suite 200
Lanham, Maryland 20706
Hamilton Books Acquisitions Department (301) 459-3366

Estover Road
Plymouth PL6 7PY
United Kingdom

All rights reserved
Printed in the United States of America
British Library Cataloging in Publication Information Available

Library of Congress Control Number: 2009935097
ISBN: 978-0-7618-4917-9 (clothbound : alk. paper)
ISBN: 978-0-7618-4918-6 (paperback : alk. paper)
eISBN: 978-0-7618-4919-3

∞™ The paper used in this publication meets the minimum
requirements of American National Standard for Information
Sciences—Permanence of Paper for Printed Library Materials,
ANSI Z39.48-1992

To Carol—Thank you for your love,
your support, and your encouragement.

Contents

In Appreciation — vii
Introduction — ix

1 Murky Waters — 1
2 Genoa — 9
3 Conversion at the Reservation School — 15
4 The Santee Normal Training School — 20
5 The World outside Nebraska, 1884–1901 — 24
6 Mount Hermon Preparatory School for Boys — 27
7 Yale — 39
8 The Roes — 44
9 Choosing Roads — 56
10 The World outside the Classroom, 1902–1910 — 71
11 Oberlin — 75
12 Auburn Theological Seminary — 82
13 The Roe Indian Institute — 87
14 Sleeping with the Enemy — 107

15	The End of the Chosen Road	113
16	What If	115
Bibliography		119
Index		123

In Appreciation

Auburn/Union Theological Seminary
Genoa Historical Museum
Haskell Indian Nations University Cultural Center and Museum
Kansas State Historical Society
Nebraska State Historical Society
Northfield Mount Hermon School Archives
Oberlin University Archives
Presbyterian Historical Society
Yale University Library
Cover photo courtesy of The Burke Library Archives (Columbia University Libraries) at Union Theological Seminary, New York.

Introduction

Henry Roe Cloud just might be one of the most important Americans you have never heard of. I had just started reading Luther Standing Bear's *Land of the Spotted Eagle* when, in the forward, I saw where Richard N. Ellis referred to Cloud and several other Native Americans as a "small but active group of highly educated Indians."[1] As a history major with an unusual interest in all things Indian, I was embarrassed but intrigued. I was even more interested when I read that Cloud was a teacher, a school administrator, and even an ordained Presbyterian minister. To a point, our lives seemed to parallel. I have been an educator, teacher and principal at the middle school and high school level. Eventually I became involved in higher education. He was a Winnebago. I am a Wannabe. I am even an ordained Presbyterian deacon and elder. However, I had never seen Henry Cloud's name in any book or article I had read in my first fifty plus years. Was the oversight mine or everybody else's?

    Actually, as I have come to realize, the story about the impact Henry Roe Cloud had on Native American education is reasonably well known. Thomas Sorci wrote that "no greater voice has been raised for the cause of education than that of Henry Roe Cloud."[2] Steven J. Crum said, "If there was a honor roll identifying 'Who's Who of Indian reform' in early twentieth-century America, Henry Roe Cloud would certainly be included."[3] In 1914 Cloud was a member of the national government's Survey Commission on Indian Education. At that same time, he investigated the general conditions of the Indian school system for the Phelps-Stokes Fund—a foundation established in 1911, to address the needs of African Americans, Native Americans, Africans and the rural and urban poor. In addition to being an ordained Presbyterian minister, he was the first Native American to graduate from

Yale. He worked with his adoptive parents, Dr. Walter C. Roe and Mary Wickham Roe to establish the Roe Indian Institute, which was later renamed the American Indian Institute. When it opened in 1915, it was the only Indian-run high school in the United States. In 1928, he coauthored *The Meriam Report,* or *The Problems of Indian Administration,* which gave attention to the myriad of problems in the areas of health, education, and general living conditions on reservations. Cloud was at least partially responsible for the report's attention to the education of Native American females—a long neglected group. In 1933, he was appointed superintendent of the Haskell Indian Institute in Lawrence, Kansas, which was the nation's largest Indian school. In 1936, he left Haskell to be the Superintendent of Indian Education At-Large with the Bureau of Indian Affairs. Cloud's reputation and stature could have easily placed him at least on the periphery of mainstream political power during the early part of the twentieth century. In fact, he likely could have been an actual power broker, but he eschewed any Native American partisanship that might seem to advance any political agenda other than the rights of Indians. He was considered a scholar, an educator, a writer, an administrator, and a politician, and his impact on Native American history should not be ignored. Therefore, the oversight had indeed been mine. I hope that this biography will prevent others from making the same mistake.

The purpose of this book is not simply to repeat information about all of his endeavors and accomplishments, but rather to look in detail at practices, events, and experiences in his own life—personal, education, and spiritual— that might have emerged later as factors that contributed to his understanding, vision and undying energy in the critical areas of education and faith. Specifically, more so than many of his Native American contemporaries, Cloud seemed to be able to reconcile the traditional teachings with those he acquired after leaving his culture of birth. He was able to translate this complicated mosaic into a value system that resulted in extraordinarily positive contributions in education, religion, and government. A person, any person, is the sum of the interactions of many variables, and Henry Cloud was no different. In fact, as are many Native Americans, he was the sum of far more variables than most.

I have chosen to arrange this book chronologically for the most part. Initially I will focus on the traditional education and belief system he knew in the Winnebago culture during his formative years. I will also chronicle his whiter experiences at the Genoa School, Santee Mission School, Mount Hermon, Yale, Oberlin, and Auburn Theological Seminary. My attention will then focus on his efforts as a teacher and educational administrator.

NOTES

1. Luther Standing Bear, *Land of the Spotted Eagle* (Lincoln: University of Nebraska Press, 1978), xiii.
2. Thomas Sorci, "Latter Day Father of the Indian Nations." *The News* 27, no. 3, (Summer 1988): 17.
3. Steven J. Crum, "Henry Roe Cloud: A Winnebago Indian Reformer; His Quest for American Indian Higher Education." *Kansas History* 11, no. 3. (1988): 171.

Chapter One

Murky Waters

In his autobiography *From Wigwam to Pulpit*, Henry Roe Cloud indicated that he was probably born in the winter of 1884.[1] Other sources, and Cloud himself on some occasions, indicated that he was born December 28, 1886, and still other said he was born in 1882 or 1883. An 1894 census gave his age as 12 indicating a likely birth year of 1882 or 1883.[2] Even if the exact year is still uncertain, we do know the place.

He was born on the Winnebago Reservation in northeast Nebraska in Thurston County. He described his earliest home as a bark wigwam, which was essentially a one-room circular building where the entire family "ate, slept, and made merry."[3] He shared the wigwam with a half-brother and sister (Susan and Anson), his mother, Hard to See, his stepfather, Nah'ilayhunkay, and occasionally his grandmother, Good Feather Woman. His parents hunted and trapped for a living. At that time, most Winnebagos either hunted and trapped, or they cut timber for the railroads. In 1910, Cloud wrote, "As I look back to my own childhood, I can hear the sound of the ring of the axe and the crash of the falling trees as they fell before the blows struck by Indian hands."[4] Although later he could speak English, Latin, and French, his initial language was that of the Winnebago—Ho-chunk—a Siouan language. He lived in Winnebago for the first seven to ten years of his life.

Henry Cloud revealed very few details about his early life, but in 1978, Anne Woesha Cloud North, his daughter, submitted her doctoral dissertation entitled "Informal Education in Winnebago Tribal Society with Implications for Formal Education" to the graduate faculty at the University of Nebraska. Her work serves to fill in many gaps left by Cloud's limited discussion of his early life—or at least those of the typical life of a Winnebago young person.[5] The family, immediate and extended, shared the responsibility of a young Winnebago's training with the entire tribe. The main parts of that training consisted of their being role models, and communicating openly, honestly, and freely with the young person. Parents, relatives, and tribal members did not divide those responsibilities. They executed them seamlessly. Ceremonies that acknowledged different stages of development represented the primary formal aspects of Winnebago training. Instead of being through direct, structured schooling as we think of it, most learning was accomplished through self-discovery or informal training that involved the child learning by means of identifying with role models, by adults sharing or demonstrating beliefs with them, and by absorbing the combined and inherited wisdom of the tribe. In other words, Winnebago youth learned through daily contact with their people and through their own relationship to nature and to their world. This description echoed the writings of Ella Deloria, who said that "traditional Indian education was done by precept and example (learning by discovery)."[6] Paul Radin stated that "the Winnebago seem to have a more or less formal system of education. This consisted of a series of precepts on different aspects of life, such as the duty of fasting, of being a warrior, of behavior to one's parents and relatives, how to treat one's wife and women in general, how to bring up children, how to behave to strangers, etc. These formal teachings were called hok-i-ku, which means 'precepts or teachings'."[7] Additionally, and significantly in terms of Cloud's life, there seemed to be a great deal of emphasis placed on the development of self-control. These Winnebago percepts re-emerge in Cloud's later writings and sermons.

The traditional education of a young Winnebago child can be described as falling under six headings: (1) Naming, (2) Storytelling, (3) Fasting and the vision quest, preparation of boys for adulthood, (4) Fasting and menses, preparation of girls for adulthood, (5) Preparation of the holy person for religious leadership, curing and healing; and (6) Preparation for a vocation. Since the locus of his education changed from the tribe to the school at a fairly early age, Cloud's description of his own early life dealt primarily with naming, storytelling, and fasting.

Although Henry Roe Cloud did not talk about his naming ceremony as a Winnebago, and writers have dealt significantly more with his name changes later in life, he did describe his name's derivation. His Indian name was Wo-Na-Xi-Lay-Hunka, which, according to Henry, meant War Chief. In fact, Cloud referred to his clan, one of the extremely influential group of Bird Clans, as the War Clan—the ultimate "deciders" about going or not going to war. He said that his name was taken from the lightening spirits, who the Winnebago believed controlled the destinies of men in war. He was named for the chief among these spirits.[8]

The Winnebago generally held the naming ceremony within ten days of the birth, but the actual time lapse seems to have varied considerably. Interestingly, if the father was not able to provide the amount of food necessary for the feast, it was often delayed. The Winnebago father could even abdicate his responsibility of sponsoring the feast and give the responsibility to the mother's clan if they were willing to accept it. In this situation, the "naming rights" would fall to her side of the family. As a child and before the naming ceremony, Cloud was referred to as Co-no-Kaw, which seems to be a fairly common generic name given to children before they received their formal name. As a young man with his ceremonially given name, Wo-Na-Xi-Lay-Hunka recognized and appreciated the connection with his ancestors. He, no doubt, observed naming ceremonies and recognized their importance as a way of establishing individual identity and relations within the extended family.

As an adult, Cloud's favorite memories from childhood were those that were associated with his grandmother's visits in the winter and with her storytelling. All summer long she refused to tell them stories, but in the winter things changed. During this cold time when the snake was in its hole, and the days were shorter, they heard the trees creak in the icy wind as they listened to her tell stories about nature, war, and heroes of their people. He said that there was always a test night, during which she required one of the young boys to retell the story she had previously told. Cloud remembered that every story had a lesson—like Biblical parables. He particularly enjoyed her stories about the trickster named Wak-Chun-Koga. (Wakdunkaga)—the central figure of a book written by Paul Radin in 1956 entitled *The Trickster: A Study in American Indian Myth.* The educational value of the Trickster, according to Radin, was that "he knows neither good nor evil yet he is responsible for both. He possesses no values, moral or social, is at the mercy of his passions and appetites, yet through his actions all values come into being."[9]

One of the first things Wo-Na-Xi-Lay-Hunka remembered learning was that when they were hungry and without food, the best course of action was to lie down and rest at such times and not to complain. Another one of his early memories was running around and around a big tree while his grandfather shot small arrows at him. He did not realize until later that his grandfather was helping him learn how to avoid the real arrows that some enemy might shoot at him. He said that he learned other practical things too, like how to use the bow and arrow and not just how to avoid being a target. He did not talk about receiving instruction in practical skills or actually being "taught" at all. Winnebago youth were not taught how to do things—even those things that might seem to be practical and useful. They were not given simple tasks that might be boring, inconsequential, or even in terms we use in differentiated education today, disrespectful. Their universal teachers challenged them at the outset to do it authentically and to use the real materials. This idea re-emerged in Cloud's life as an educator and school administrator.

Wo-Na-Xi-Lay-Hunka's uncles, as is true in most avuncular clan relationships, were not only responsible for punishment for his bad behavior but also for his spiritual training. His grandmother had twelve children, and one of his uncles taught him what he called "the art of worship." His uncle would take him to the banks of the river where he would make offerings of tobacco, feathers, and oak twigs to the river and to fire. Significantly, his uncle never made an obvious effort to tell him what the ceremonies meant or why they made the offerings—just as his grandfather's arrow lessons were experienced and not discussed. Understanding came later.

During his youth, Wo-Na-Xi-Lay-Hunka became familiar with the basic precepts of Winnebago spirituality or religion. Radin said that 'the Indian does not interpret life in terms of religion, but religion in terms of life." He went on to say that the Winnebago possessed no disinterested, unselfish love for any spirit or deity to whom he might pray, except in situations when there might be some significant crisis or when it might work to his immediate advantage. He described Winnebago religion as being largely devoid in any belief of a single higher magical supernatural power. Anything that a Winnebago described as sacred essentially was called that because it potentially had the power to bestow some blessing. To the average Winnebago the world was occupied by an indefinite number of spirits who manifested their existence in many ways. They might be visible, audible, felt emotionally, or they could manifest themselves by some sign or result. The basic, underlying religious concept of the Winnebago, as well as Lakota, Algonquin, and many others, was the belief in the existence of a magical power in animate and inanimate objects. This belief led to their understanding that there were in fact people who possess supernatural power as well. The most important deities of the Winnebago and what was called the Medicine Lodge were the Earthmaker, Sun, Moon, Earth, Morning Star, Disease-giver, Thunderbird, Trickster, Bladder, Turtle, He-who-wears-heads-as-earrings, and the Hare, and Waterspirit. Feasting and fasting comprised the two principal elements of worship.[10]

This description differs somewhat from one given in 1915 in a book entitled *In Camp and Tepee: An Indian Mission Story* written by Elizabeth M. Page. In this book, published by the Board of Publication and Bible School Work of the Reformed Church in America, the author said that "among the Winnebagoes there is a belief that all the spirits and supernatural beings of the earth and the underworld are subject to one Great Spirit."[11] Writing nearly ninety years later in 2003, Bonnie Sue Lewis said essentially the same thing. She said, "Winnebago society likewise, reflected similar values and further illustrates the way biblical and Native Values complemented each other."[12] In the preface to her book, Page said that she was deeply indebted to "Rev. Henry Roe Cloud for advice and careful criticism of the chapters on Winnebago."[13] However, as a student at Yale, Cloud wrote an article for *The*

Christian Intelligencer about the Medicine Lodge and its part in Winnebago religion that included a quote from Dr. A. L. Riggs that said, "If you convert those Winnebagos to Christianity it will mean that the religion of Jesus Christ can save any Indian Tribe," and one from Dr. Walter Roe that said, "The Winnebagos are a very hard people to reach." Cloud himself described the Winnebago civilization as emerging from "the darkness of superstition and vice."[14] In talking about a great Spirit, Page was referring to Mâ'ûna (the Earthmaker) who has otherwise been generally described as distant and disassociated rather than being one great controlling spirit. Earthmaker was referred to as the Great Spirit, but never appeared to mortals in any but a symbolic form, and he never intervened in human affairs, except for one important function: those who resisted all temptations to remain in any of the several paradises of the afterlife and made it to the lodge of Earthmaker, were given an audience by the deity and might be reborn on earth to any parents they choose. These spiritually qualified people might, in fact, earn reincarnation several times, they might choose to be reborn pretty much as they were or as an animal, the opposite sex, or a white person. Page probably invoked the Great Spirit image to make the leap from traditional Winnebago beliefs to Christianity seem like it was not such a great one—despite what Cloud, Roe, and Riggs had said earlier. She also acknowledged that the darker side of their belief system, as represented in the Medicine Lodge, was certainly not strange to young Wo-Na-Xi-Lay-Hunka (Cloud) because his mother was a "medicine-woman" who was held in high esteem. Cloud himself talked about the Medicine Lodge in the article in "The Christian Intelligencer."

> No justice has been done to Medicine Lodge by this bare outline, but it is given to show what unspeakable heathenism and crime it fosters. Medicine Lodge to the Indian people themselves has become a synonym for death. Even in it purity it was a terror to the tribe, for it claims to have in its keeping the welfare of the life that now is, and the life in the hereafter. It is not hard to see how in its present form it has become the scourge and doom of the Winnebago people. In the same manner in which the Roman Catholic Church sold indulgences in the early days, the Medicine Lodge chiefs sell indulgences. Punishments are meted out by secret poisons. Immunity from punishments is bought by life-long service to the Medicine Lodge chief. At stated seasons they give him food, clothing, horses, dogs for sacrifice, and in these days, firewater, to curry favor and to propitiate his wrath. . . . All live in fear of the Medicine Lodge and all subordinate spirits. All live in fear of the Medicine Lodge chiefs, who are believed to be representatives of the spirit of the universe.[15]

To me, the gap between traditional Winnebago religion and Christianity appears to be very wide, making Cloud's conversion and commitment even more extraordinary.

The Winnebago had a decidedly unchristian view of death and the afterlife. Because the Winnebago religion idealized war, the best death was one that resulted directly from war. The other acceptable cause of death was simply old age. The Winnebago referred to this type of death as being as coming from crumbling bones (osteoporosis?). Witchcraft or breaking taboos caused most of the other deaths. Although occasionally deaths were simply accidental, and they meant nothing at all. There have been stories that the Winnebago scaffolded the dead, but they had used burial for an extremely long time. They believed that the decedent remained present as a spirit during a four-night wake. After that, she/he was directed to start the difficult journey to the next world. In traditional Winnebago religion, the next world was seen as an idealized or perfected version of life on earth. Wo-Na-Xi-Lay-Hunka was born and spent the early years of his life in this religious system, and his leap to Christianity was a huge one.

Fasting was a topic Cloud discussed extensively in his writings throughout his life. It is clear that he practiced it in the traditional Winnebago setting. Regarding the Lakota, who were related to the Winnebago, Deloria said, "I cannot give any one fasting experience in detail here. They were all very holy, and they were all very involved. They were remembered with photographic clarity, and took a very long while to tell."[16] Fasting was one of the ways a young man could establish an honorable place among the members of his tribe. Cloud says that he "often took part" in fasts, and acknowledged that "an Indian child pleases his parents most when he fasts, for by it, it is believed that he secures benefits far greater than they can bestow."[17] It was also felt that fasting helped prepare them for times "when the earth was narrow" or times were hard. In his address entitled "An Anthropologist's View of Reservation Life" he repeated this idea by saying that "the greatest ambition of every Indian family was to have their boys and even girls seek the presence of super naturals through fasting and dreams. . . Well do I remember the times my older brother and I after blackening our faces with charcoal and having fasted for several days, climbing trees and thus perched high up, watched for our father's appearance in the far distance." Asking and answering his own question: "Why do we stress this phase of primitive life?" he says that "the answer is that no one can really understand Indian culture who does not know by deep study or personal experience this great fundamental." However, he admitted that he and his brother often just "two hungry boys," and that they never had a dream or vision at all.[18]

In 1914, in an address at the Lake Mohonk Conference on the Indian and Other Dependent Peoples, Cloud said," Education unrelated to life is of no use. Education is the leading-out process of the young until they themselves know what they are best fitted for in life. Education is for complete living;

that is, the educational process must involve the heart, head, and hand. . . . We cannot pay exclusive attention to the education of one part and afford to let the other part or parts suffer."[19] While his exposure to aspects of the heart, head, and hand of the Winnebago might have been limited, clearly the learning he received before he made his journey to the Genoa Indian School, and into white culture for the first time, had an impact on his perception of education and religion. Miles and years away from his "bark wigwam on the banks of the murky waters," he addressed the influence this early education had on him. In 1941, less than 10 years before his death he reflected about "the majesty of the Indian mind, its breadth of concept, and its inherent beauty."[20]

Wo-Na-Xi-Lay-Hunka spent the first few years of his life in a traditional Winnebago setting. From that culture, he learned the value of active learning as opposed to didactic instruction. Learning involved discovery and was experiential—not passive. Young people were allowed to, even encouraged to, make mistakes. Wo-Na-Xi-Lay-Hunka grew up watching for lessons rather than being overtly taught. As a result he was observant, perceptive, and active—qualities that served him well later in life. He learned about traditions and connections (to people, nature, and spirits) from ceremonies—lessons that contributed to an appreciation of liturgy and corporate worship. He saw adults playing and having fun. He watched and perhaps participated in the kicking game, the moccasin game, the tree game, and the cup-and-ball game. He began to acquire the practical skills by "the doing"—features that helped shape his ideas about teaching and pedagogy in general. He learned the importance of self-control, self-discipline, and self-sacrifice. He learned that fasting, apart from being spiritually satisfying, was also a way of putting his people in a position which would enable them to stoically deal with the inevitable crises in life, which was reasonable to believe might take place—things that would help as Native Americans and oppressed minorities in general walked the long road to equality. Practicality and self-discipline prevailed in education and spirituality.

NOTES

1. Henry Roe Cloud, "From Wigwam to Pulpit," *Missionary Review of the World*, (May 1915): 3.

2. Jason M.Tetzloff, "To Do Some Good Among the Indians: Henry Roe Cloud and Twentieth Century Native American Advocacy." (doctoral dissertation, Perdue University, 1996), 8.

3. Cloud, "From Wigwam to Pulpit," 3.

4. Henry Roe Cloud, "An Appeal to Christian People," Lake Mohonk Conference, October 19, 1910.

5. Woesha Cloud North, "Informal Education in Winnebago Tribal Society with Implications for Formal Education," (doctoral dissertation, The University of Nebraska, 1978), 9.

6. Ella Deloria, *Speaking of Indians,* (Lincoln: University of Nebraska Press, 1998), 63.

7. Paul Radin, *The Winnebago Tribe,* (Lincoln: University of Nebraska Press, 1990), 118.

8. Cloud, "From Wigwam to Pulpit," 7.

9. Paul Radin, *The Trickster: A Study in American Indian Mythology,* (New York: Schocken Books, 1956), xxiii.

10. Radin, *The Winnebago Tribe*, 229.

11. Elizabeth M.Page, *In Camp and Tepee,* (New York: Fleming H. Revell Company, 1915), 186.

12. Bonnie Sue Lewis, *Creating Christian Indians,* (Norman: University of Oklahoma Press, 2003), 39.

13. Page, *In Camp and Tepee*, 7.

14. Henry Roe Cloud,"The Winnebago Medicine Lodge," *The Christian Intelligencer,* (December 22, 1909): 833.

15. Ibid., 833.

16. Deloria, *Speaking of Indians*, 60.

17. Cloud, "From Wigwam to Pulpit," 5.

18. Henry Roe Cloud, "An Antropologist's View of Reservation Life," Address at the *Northwest, Inter-mountain, and Montana Superintendent's Conference,* (Pendleton, September 11, 1941).

19. Henry Roe Cloud, "Education of the American Indian," Lake Mohonk Conference, 1914.

20. Cloud, "An Antropologist's View of Reservation Life."

Chapter Two

Genoa

There are numerous descriptive accounts of life in Indian boarding schools. Most of them, like *Education for Extinction*[1] by David Wallace Adams describe this "great experiment" far better than I can. Indeed it is ironic that a nation whose very government was once called a "great experiment" would attempt to essentially enslave a people and destroy a culture using the same title. My accounts and descriptions will focus only on those schooling experiences of Henry Cloud and on accounts, data, and resources specific to them.

In 1892, when Wo-Na-Xi-Lay-Hunka was seven (or nine or ten) years old he and his brother were taken to a non-reservation school in Genoa, Nebraska, about a hundred miles from their home. Wo-Na-Xi-Lay-Hunka said that "an Indian policeman came to take my brother" to school.[2] Actually he described it as going to "see some writing," which was a literal translation. He persuaded his mother to let him go along—not so much to see the writing as to be with his brother. Later, Cloud minimized the importance of the occasion by saying that all he really remembered about the school was that "I herded sheep, flew kites, fought John Hunter, slid in winter, caught a groundsquirrel and a young crow for pets, stole grapes and cherries in summer, and once went to the hospital with a big splinter in my foot."[3]

The Genoa Indian Industrial School opened on February 20, 1884, in Nance County, Nebraska, on the grounds of an earlier vocational training school for Indian children. Located in the Loup River valley, it was the fourth non-reservation boarding institution established by the Office of Indian Affairs. The town of Genoa was selected because the Federal Government already owned the former Pawnee Reservation property there. Mormon missionaries founded he town in 1857. It was one of several settlements the Church of Jesus Christ of Latter Day Saints had established to serve as way stations for the Brigham Young Express and Carrying Company, which had the government mail contract to Salt Lake City, and they also served as rest and supply stops for believers traveling across the Plains to Salt Lake City. In 1859, Federal Government forced the Mormons to abandon Genoa when the settlement became part of the Pawnee Indian Reservation. Genoa served as the Pawnee Indian Agency until 1876, when the Pawnee were removed to the Indian Territory, and the reservation lands became available for other uses by the federal government. The local citizens actually collected money and contributed $500.00 to the government to help it buy addition land for the institute. The students who eventually came to the Genoa Indian School were from 10 states and over 20 tribes. When Wo-Na-Xi-Lay-Hunka started school, there were approximately 300 students. The school grew from the first 74 students to an enrollment of close to 600, and its campus ultimately had over 30 buildings on 640 acres.

The Genoa Indian School, referred to sometimes as the Grant Institute, featured a basic curriculum. The primary academic concern was teaching the students English. Instruction level was determined by ability rather than age, and reading, writing, arithmetic were the curricular mainstays. Half of the day was spent in class and the other half in assigned trades. Genoa lacked the strong academic reputation some of the other schools had, but it was not without its admirers. In the June 5, 1891 edition of the school newspaper, *The Pipe of Peace,* a "Brief but Bright 'Write-up' by the Big Brother of the *Columbus Sentinel* was published.

> It is worth a two-days' journey on horse-back to visit Institute and take observations of the methods employed to rear the bronzed-faced children of the noble red man in the arts of civilization. Many of our readers have visited this school, but those who have not might be interested in knowing something concerning it.. . . it has come to be generally accepted among statesmen and philanthropists, and it has come to be the generally accepted belief that "education" is the only humane solution, end, moreover, it is cheaper than any other method of dealing with the scattered remnants of our aboriginal brethren. To accomplish this purpose eleven educational institutions have been established and are maintained at government expense, the largest is at Carlisle Pa. The school at Genoa is third in importance and bids fair to rank first within a very short time, having advantages of location and healthful surroundings not possessed by any of the others.
>
>   . . . Last Monday through the courtesy of Supt. Backus the Sentinel was permitted the freedom of the premises, and noted with pleasure the perfect system upon which the school is conducted in its educational and industrial departments. In the first place, the utmost order and neatness prevails throughout the entire institution, and perfect discipline is maintained. The different departments of the school are under the immediate supervision of competent instructors, and many students show wonderful proficiency in their studies. The industrial departments, which are very important in the matter of fitting the boys for use-

ful avocations, are something of a wonder, and to show what they amount to it is only necessary to state that in the past year the harness shop turned out 170 sets of the best double harnesses and 185 common. The broom factory shows a record of 1,000 dozen floor brooms and 100 dozen whisk brooms, all the work of Indian boys. The shoe shop produced 297 pairs of assorted shoes and did a large amount of repairing besides. The tailor lads made 76 complete suits of clothes, 270 pairs of pants, 145 coats, and 24 heavy aprons for the school, besides several suits for outsiders. A wagon and blacksmith shop is also entitled to notice, as the boys have just completed the first wagon, which will bear the most critical inspection. . . . Much more of interest could be written concerning this school and the peculiarities of the pupils, but space forbids. But we venture the prediction that if the loyal and untiring efforts of Supt. W.B. Backus count for what they are worth, Grant Institute will, in a short time, be at the head of the Indian Industrial schools of America.[4]

Another article written at the end of July in *The Pipe of Peace* reported that it (Genoa) was "among the most important schools of its class in the United States, or for that matter perhaps in the world, ranking third in attendance but second to none in the active and effective part it is taking in solving the much mooted 'Indian question'."[5] It is obvious that at Genoa, the answer to the Indian question involved the elimination of native language, assimilation into the white culture, and learning a viable trade. As these articles show, the primary pursuits of the school were vocational in nature, but recreation and sports played a part as well. Genoa competed interscholastically in several areas including debate, tennis, boys and girls basketball, football, and baseball. Additionally ice skating was popular. The school had a well developed intramural program as well and entertained students by occasional trips to the circus. It is highly likely that Wo-Na-Xi-Lay-Hunka participated in the sports program, and he later excelled at sports at other schools. It is also likely that he was in the band. Just a couple of years after he left Genoa it is recorded that he played the coronet.

The glowing editorial from *The Sentinel* notwithstanding, it is obvious that Genoa had its share of problems and issues while Wo-Na-Xi-Lay-Hunka attended. The school attempted an "outing" program very loosely patterned after General Pratt's at Carlisle in Pennsylvania. Designed to assist Native American students in becoming more acquainted with white culture through direct contacts, at Genoa the program seemed to be more concerned with providing laborers for farmers in the area as well as for providing house servants in the city. The school found itself embroiled in a labor dispute with competing beet growers in Colorado when it appeared that they were going to "out" several students to help with the harvest there. The school received a meager $167.00 per student per year for support. Consequentially, much of what the school came to be about was to supplement their operating funds. This was done by selling the surplus from their gardens and dairy, participating in open commerce with the community through other industrial endeavors, the direct hiring out of labor, and most unfortunately, in cutting as many costs as possible.

In his annual report to the Commissioner of Indian Affairs in Washington for 1891, the superintendent reported:

> A pleasant variety of food at the children's table is due to fresh eggs, abundances of milk and butter, which now supplies the whole school. The farm furnishes the best of vegetables and never has the school fared better than the present time. This variety of good food has proven healthful for the children, and the excellent sanitary conditions of the school during the past year may be partly owing to this condition. Only one death has occurred among the girls during the year—that of one very delicate child who was unable to rally from a severe attack of La Grippe. Sore eyes are quite rare among them, and the Matron reports having been called up by illness only one night during the whole year. This better condition of health may be attributed to a greater degree of cleanliness and personal attention, the importance of which they are daily taught to observe. The bath facilities are very good, but could be better. (Later in the report, after a thorough description and accounting of the efforts in the sewing room, harness shop, broom factory, shoe shop, carpenter shop, blacksmith and wagon shop, paint shop, and the school's 43 "milch cows," the superintendent picked back up on the sanitation and health topic.)
>
> The health of the pupils during the first half of the year was exceedingly good. About that time La Grippe seized upon us and continued until late in spring. It was particularly severe upon those affected with scrofula and also those who either had consumption fully developed or were in the first stages. One child had inflammation of the brain and died. A summary of the records for the year shows the following: Severe cases of scrofula, 11; consumption, 15; sore eyes, 38; mumps, 38; inflammation of the brain, 1; chorea, 2; erysipelas, 1. Besides the above there were numerous cases that required and received treatment; but being of such minor importance were not recorded.
>
> . . . The tendency in this locality, both among whites and Indians, is toward recovery from all acute diseases, except such as are regarded almost certainly of a fatal character, and fortunately we have never been visited with any diseases of a malignant and contagious nature since the organization of the school.[6]

If that was true, things were about to change. Wo-Na-Xi-Lay-Hunka arrived at Genoa before the people in the township started providing the school with water. Their source was a well operated by a windmill that pumped water into a 300 gallon storage tank. From there it flowed to the kitchens and washrooms in the school—the same facilities the superintendent admitted could stand some improvement. Communicable diseases became common. Measles killed 10 in 1892, Wo-Na-Xi-Lay-Hunka's year of arrival, and was the likely cause of his cousin, Fred Hensley's, death there. Tuberculosis was also common. Twenty-three students died of TB between 1884 and 1894.

Wo-Na-Xi-Lay-Hunka's lack of enthusiasm was probably tied more to the educational program than anything else or to a sense of isolation. He talked about being "thrown in with Sioux, Omahas, Apaches, Pottawatomies, Ottoes, Arappahoes, and Cheyennes who could not speak Winnebago."[7] He certainly did not realize at the time that this was done deliberately to help kill off the use of native languages and to develop English as a common language. He probably also had a difficult time understanding the practice of requiring students to write letters home to their parents every month. Someone of his insight probably saw the folly in writing letters to people who could not read them. However, this letter writing was a common practice in Indian schools and was seen as a way of honing practical English skills. The students were also encouraged to write to various "pen pals" in eastern cities. These letters were always reviewed and carefully screened to make sure the school was represented in a positive way. Several series of letters seemed to been exchanged with a young girls' religious club in the Boston area called the Golden Rule Circle of King's Daughters and the In-as-Much Circle.. Letters from one of its members—Bessie Tripp were published in *The Pipe of Peace*.

> Dear Friend: I have been looking over your last letter, and as I have an opportunity will try to answer it. The only fault that I find with your letters, they are so short. Very interesting, I must admit, what there is to them. . . Do you expect to go to your home this summer? You have never told me what part of Dakota you live in. I would like to know. How many rooms are there in the main building of Grant Institute? What color is the outside? Are there many buildings around it. Or does it standby itself almost? If these questions tire you, simply ignore them, but if you feel disposed to gratify my curiosity, I should like to hear all you can say about those things. Just tell me in a simple way, as if you were talking to me.[8]

It almost seems like Bessie was aware that she was getting a somewhat abridged version of life at Genoa. Contact with the refined girls in eastern cities was intended to expand their minds and help them to grasp new ideas and subjects that were "unknown to their ancestors." Three circles of the King's Daughters were formed at the school—the Golden Rule Circle, the Watch Circle, and the Little Pick-Ups Circle. Superintendent Backus said that the formation of the circles "has had a good and refining influence over all."[9]

Wo-Na-Xi-Lay-Hunka's memories of his years at Genoa might seem vague. Perhaps he was not challenged academically. The institution's philosophy that an industrial education was far superior to an academic one might have proven to be true during his early years. Later, with more than a hint of resentment, Henry Roe Cloud said, "I worked two years in turning a washing machine to reduce the running experiences of the institution. It did not take me long to learn how to run the machine, and the rest of the two years I nursed a growing hatred for it."[10] Maybe the childhood memories of flying kites, herding sheep, fighting, and sliding in the winter are really the most important ones after all. Regardless, after he had been at Genoa for two years his people came to take him and his brother home. That was the only other mention of his brother at the school. As they rode the 100 or so miles back home, Wo-Na-Xi-Lay-Hunka probably thought about what he had lost at Genoa. He lost his cousin. He lost his native language. He and his father could not even talk to each other on their journey. As is true for every child going for school for the first time, he probably lost some of his innocence. However, at the same time, he had to be aware of what he had gained. He had seen some writing. He would soon be able to use that new language and that writing for the betterment of other Native Americans. In a month or so he had regained his language and was able to use it and the Winnebago culture to add depth, eloquence, and meaning to his later writings, sermons, and speeches. He lost his Indian name and received a new one. His place in, and yet between, the Native American and white world was solidifying. Wo-Na-Xi-Lay-Hunka enrolled at Genoa Indian School and Henry Clarence Cloud left it.

NOTES

1. David Wallace Adams, *Education for Extinction*, (Lawrence: University Press of Kansas, 1995).
2. Henry Roe Cloud, "From Wigwam to Pulpi," *Missionary Review of the World*, (May 1915): 7.
3. Cloud, "From Wigwam to Pulpit," 8.
4. "About Grant Institute," *The Pipe of Peace*, (Genoa, Nebraska, June 5, 1891): 1.
5. "Regarding the Indian School," *The Pipe of Peace*. (Genoa, Nebraska, July 31, 1891).
6. W.B. Backus, Superintendent, "Third Annual Report," *The Pipe of Peace*. (Genoa, Nebraska, August Friday, 1891).
7. Cloud, "From Wigwam to Pulpit," 7.
8. Bessie Tripp, "Bessie Tripp's Letter," *The Pipe of Peace*, (Genoa, Nebraska, May 16 Friday, 1891): 2.
9. W.B. Backus, Superintendent, "Third Annual Report," *The Pipe of Peace*, (Genoa, Nebraska, August Friday, 1891).
10. Frederick Hoxie, *Talking Back to Civilization: Indian Voices from the Progressive Era*, (New York: Bedford/St. Martin's, 2001), 61.

Chapter Three

Conversion at the Reservation School

It was not long after Henry Cloud returned home that an Indian policeman took him to another school. The Indian agent at Winnebago and his police were remarkably diligent in making sure that the young people were in school. Officials in the federal government were completely convinced that education was the only effective way to achieve their goal of assimilation. There was an economic incentive as well—the number of students attending each school determined how much money the schools received. The government was struggling with developing the most efficient educational system or structure for the Indians. At the time Henry attended school, there were separate day schools on the reservations, reservation boarding schools, and the off-reservation boarding schools. The consensus was that the day schools were the least effective since they allowed students to return home every day. The issue of relapse was always a matter of concern. One agent described the day schools as being a "total waste."[1] Indian parents were not always interested in having their children attend school. Often agents either threatened to, or actually did, withhold rations. Other devises were used or discussed that would isolate the schools from the tribe. Vacations or visitations were limited and they built fences or adobe walls around the schools. Increasingly, it became apparent that the most practical measure was to move schools father away from the reservations.

Henry attended the Winnebago Reservation School, or Winnebago Industrial School, in near-by Macy, Nebraska. This school permitted occasional weekend trips back home, but otherwise it was fairly typical of most reservation boarding schools. In 1894, a reporter for the *Milwaukee Sentinel* described the Tomah Reservation School, which had been created in Wisconsin also for Winnebago youth.

The boys are taught to become model farmers and carpenters, etc. They are taught to plow, to harrow, to plant, to hoe, to weed, to care for the tools, the stock, the horses, the barn, to harvest, to store the harvest, to make their own beds, and keep their rooms in order; in fact, to do everything needful and helpful about the farm and house. A detail of boys is made in like manner as with the girls, for such lines of work as are specifically adapted to them. Each detail holds for two weeks. These work at their respective duties half the day and are in the school room half the day during school hours.[2]

Henry described his days at the reservation school much as he did the time he spent at Genoa. He remembered riding ponies, shooting bows and arrows, playing marbles, racing, jumping, swimming, and throwing the sumach-sticks. It is interesting to note that these seem to be more traditional in nature than the activities at Genoa. Cloud is either suggesting that there was a little less supervision and restriction against all things Indian or, more likely, he was setting the stage to compare this activities with the things he did after his conversion to Christianity. Henry was adept at playing marbles and recalled frequently "playing for keeps." After he won marbles from other students, he would the sell them back and was always able to have a little money on hand.

Although he again did not seem to be overly impressed with his education there, or with its rigid structure, Henry did experience what he called the "greatest event of my life" at the reservation school. That was his conversion to Christianity. Religious training was part of the curriculum at government boarding schools. Like learning language and a vocation, governmental officials and philanthropists saw it as a tool that was essential for assimilation and civilization. The students regularly attended chapel during the week as well as Sunday school and church on Sunday. Henry obviously enjoyed Sundays at the school. He had started playing the cornet and had the opportunity to lead the parade of students to the church on what they called Cross Day.

One of Henry's Sunday school teachers was Mrs. Findley. In addition to having the students read about famous Biblical characters, she used a type of picture card that had information and pictures of that person on it. Henry recalled that one Sunday she was talking about the question Pontius Pilate asked after Jesus had been arrested—"What shall I do, then, with Jesus who is called Christ?" She personalized the question and asked the students, "What would you do with Jesus?" Henry's response was, "I would like to be his friend."[3] Mrs. Findley must have been impressed. She passed his response on to her husband, Reverend William T. Findley, the Presbyterian missionary to the Winnebago. For all of his dedication and hard work, Findley could hardly be described as being a very successful missionary among the Winnebago—if success was measured in numbers of converts. Henry called Findley's years of efforts "sixteen years of apparently fruitless toil."[4] However, the conversion of Henry Clarence Cloud was a significant and far-reaching one.

The story of that conversion is a somewhat bizarre, but nevertheless, extremely moving episode in Henry's life. Sleepless, frustrated and discouraged, Findley was searching for answers when he recalled the young man his wife had talked about. He felt that he could not wait any longer and went directly to the school to talk with Henry. All of the young men were asleep, and it was past midnight. The reluctant dorm supervisor asked him to wait until morning, but Findley could not be dissuaded. A few minutes later the sleepy and confused twelve-year old was brought to him. Henry recognized him as the Presbyterian minister who had preached at the church and who had, in fact, visited his family and village. Saying nothing, Findley took him outside where they sat down in the grass and they talked about Jesus Christ. Despite having gone to the Sunday school and listening to the minister's message on Cross Day, Henry had never felt any personal connection to the story. Findley artfully used Henry's description of a relation with Christ as a friendship to personalize his message, and Henry adopted this new "spirit-friend." Cloud explained in his autobiography that friendship was both a very structured and a very important concept for Native Americans.

> Friendship-making is a meaningful and very formal act among Indians. I knew that James Rain was my friend. We slept together, we played together, and fought each other. On some "Cross Day" afternoons I took him to my home, and on others he took me to his home. His family was mine, and mine was his. James Rain, I love to this day. So, I understood that when I took Jesus that night to be my friend, we were to stand by each other through this life and throughout the "land of the setting sun." He was to defend me, and I was to defend Him. I did not understand much else that Mr. Findley said that night, but I knew that I had entered upon a new life. The boys saw the changes that came over me, and I had become what the Indians called, "A Preaching Listener."[5]

Henry told the story about his conversion repeatedly, and it was obviously the watershed event in his life. Like most such events, it was not without its costs. Everyone noticed the changes. He no longer fought, and he stopped playing marbles for keeps after the preacher asked him where he got the money he was putting in the offering plate at church. He avoided tribal rituals and ceremonies and he joined a small organization called the Band of Mercy, which promised not to kill or harm any animals. Those last two changes subjected him to immediate and severe ridicule from other Indians including his own brother. Henry saw all of these as tests. His beloved grandmother told him a story.

Years ago, wearers of long broadcloth (Jesuit priests) came among the Crows and began to preach. In the course of time, a Crow Indian listened and became a "preaching listener." When the Crow Indian died the whole tribe gathered together to decide whether they should dress him in Indian fashion for "the land of the setting sun" or should put on him the robes of the strangers. They finally clothed him in black like unto his white leaders, laid him on a high booth, and went up stream to hunt. In the meantime the soul of the Indian began his last travel. He soon came to a place where the road parted, one road leading to the left and the other to the right. He took the right road, and before long, saw, in the distance the glory of some great habitation like that of the lighted heavens over some great city at night. The voices that he heard indicated that they were beings like himself, and his heart leaped within him for joy. But when he came near, he was told to go back with the words, "You have mistaken your road. This is the white man's heaven. Go back and take the other road." He was a white man in dress, but his Indian features betrayed him. Sad at heart, he returned to the parting of the ways, and taking the left-hand road soon heard sounds that cheered his heart even more than what he had seen on the road to the right. He recognized the Indian songs of this new gathering-place. When he hurried to join them he was, however, sent back by the herald of the place saying: Go back. You have mistaken your road. This is the Indian heaven." His clothes made him look like a white man. There was nothing left for the poor Indian to do but to take that road that back to his body. As he reached the place where his body was lying the tribe returned from their hunt, and on examining his body found life was in him. An old medicine woman tended to him, and when he was able to sit up he opened his mouth and told his story. "Now," said my grandmother, "I do not command you to stop being a 'a preaching listener', but if you want to be forever a wanderer in the other world, you can continue in the road you have taken."[6]

Cloud deeply valued the teaching aspects of his grandmother's stories, and surely this one caused him think about his decision. He confessed that he had a period of intense soul struggling, but in the end answered the minister's question about who he should obey first, Christ or his parents and relatives with a resounding, "Christ." He went on to say that his understanding and belief in the idea of friendship, and all it encompassed, transcended a desire to go to any particular place in the afterlife.

Within a year of his conversion, Henry's mother, father, and grandmother all died. The agency superintendent appointed "Honest John" Nunn as his guardian. But now in many respects he was all alone. He had separated himself from his tribe. He had alienated his bother. He was the only Winnebago preaching listener in the school. The other Indians called him "queer,"[7] which at the time had no homosexual implications. All of the elements were there for depression or at least for a generous amount of self-pity. During his exile, he read a Testament Findley had given him the night of his midnight visit. Instead of questioning the wisdom of his new friendship, Henry became even more convinced that he had made the right decision. He described this time in his life as "soul-loneliness" that gave way to strength and "more than a complement of deep joy."[8] William T. Findley's sole convert among the Winnebago proved to be a committed and important one.

Henry stayed at the reservation boarding school until 1898 or 1899. Reverend Findley persuaded him and seven of the other boys at the school to go to the Santee Normal Training School located about a hundred miles away in northeastern Nebraska. Henry's world had expanded roughly a hundred miles southwest from his home to Genoa and now a hundred miles northwest to Santee.

NOTES

1. David Wallace Adams, *Education for Extinction,* (Lawrence: University Press of Kansas, 1995), 29.
2. C.D. Woodruff, "Tomah Indian school," *The Milwaukee Sentinel,* 22 July 1894.
3. Henry Roe Cloud, "From Wigwam to Pulpit," *Missionary Review of the World,* (May 1915), 9.
4. Cloud, Henry Roe. "The Winnebago Medicine Lodge," *The Christian Intelligencer,* (December 22, 1909): 833.
5. Cloud, "From Wigwam to Pulpit," 9.
6. Ibid., 9.
7. Ibid., 11.
8. Ibid., 11.

Chapter Four

The Santee Normal Training School

Henry Cloud was not the only famous Native American to attend school at Santee. He followed in the footsteps of Ohiyesa, who walked over 150 miles to enroll there in 1874—four years after the school was founded. Ohiyesa later was known as Charles Eastman—a famous Indian physician, public figure, and writer. The school Ohiyesa saw was very different from the one Cloud and the seven other Winnebago boys arrived at in 1899. What had started out as little more than a log cabin that served as the school and the chapel. It grew very quickly to include 18 different buildings that housed the different departments and programs of the school. Initially it was established as a missionary effort of an association that included both the Congregationalist and Presbyterian churches. A division of the association later resulted in the Congregationalist church assuming total responsibility.

Santee was a curious hybrid. First, it was both a boarding school and a day school. The school handbook, *Woonspe-Wankantus,* listed nine day students in 1901.[1] That number fluctuated over the years. Second, initially the school was funded both by the mission association and the federal government. The support of the government stopped because ideological differences in 1893. Like other Indian schools its curriculum was divided into a vocational half and an academic half. But, at Santee, there was a great deal of emphasis placed on the academic portion of the program. The November, 1890 edition of the school newspaper, *The Word Carrier,* went so far as to say, "With the mechanical arts the object is not trade training but 'manu-mental" instruction, development of the mind and character through the hand and body. Blacksmithing, carpentering, printing are used for their mental and ethical value: a means to all around development." That same article reported that, "In academic work the pedagogical developments at Santee are not only abreast of the times, but often advance into originality."[2] The school's professional development at that time involved having the faculty study and discuss the writings and teachings of John Dewey at the University of Chicago. Each faculty member had been given a copy of a book Dewey and Laura Runyan had edited—The *Elementary School Record.* The ideas of these progressive educators were seen as being essential since, "it is sufficiently difficult to teach Indian pupils even by the very best methods. Moreover, we believe that it is not right for a missionary school to be of any kind but the best. . . ."[3]

Another reason that Santee stood virtually alone among the Indian schools of the day was that its founder, Alfred L. Riggs, insisted that it was critical to use the native language in instruction. This was in direct opposition to the position taken by the federal government, which was the total eradication of the native tongue. This difference in philosophy ended the tenuous relationship between the two. According to Ohiyesa, even the partial use of English was responsible for angst among the Indians.

> For a whole week we youthful warriors were held up and harassed with words of those letters. Like raspberry bushes in the path, they tore, they bled, and sweated us—those little words rat, eat, and so forth until not a semblance of our native dignity and self-respect was left. And we were of just the age when the Indian youth is most on his dignity! Imagine the same fellows turned loose against Custer or Harney with anything like equal numbers and weapons, and those tired generals would feel like boys! We had been bred and trained to those things; but when we found ourselves within four walls and set to pick out words of three letters we were like novices upon snow-shoes—often flat on the ground.[4]

Henry certainly found Santee to be more to his liking. Like many other students they he was influenced by the powerful convictions and personality of its founder. Alfred Riggs was the son of Stephen R. Riggs who was an extremely successful and influential missionary himself. His goal at Santee was neither that of a missionary or a preacher. There was certainly a theological element to the instruction there, but his primary goal was to open up the world of higher education to the students there. He wanted to prepare teachers and leaders. In 1916, Henry Roe Cloud wrote that "we can not think of "Zitkadan Washtay" (Riggs's Indian name meaning Good Bird) as dead. He liveth to greater endeavor, carrying out God's continuing purposes. He left the world far better than he found it, and the memory of his good works is enshrined in the hearts of red men and women, who are better happier and happier because of him."[5]

Henry's initial impressions of Santee were probably not as positive as the ones he had when he left. When the Winnebago boys arrived, one of the first things they saw from the higher elevations around the school was the "murky waters" of the Missouri River. They knew that it was the same river that flowed by their homes in Winnebago. Six of the boys left almost immediately, and in less than two weeks, Cloud was the only one left. Henry walked along for a while with the last boy to leave in the dark. That boy later told Henry that he was torn between staying and leaving and that if Henry had said something as simple as "stay around and give it more time" that he would have done that. In his autobiography Henry said that he tried to persuade him to stay. What that boy probably did not know was that Henry was feeling pretty much the same way. He admitted that there was a "fight within me"[6] at that same time. Having conquered this indecision, he resolved to return, learn as much as he could, and he reaffirmed his belief that there was more working in his life than just the power of a human.

A little more is known about what Henry did and studied at Santee than at Genoa or the reservation school. We know that he worked as a printer. A few years before Henry was in school at Santee, Riggs had presented the printing instructor there, James W. Garvie, with the task of translating a short outline of the life of Abraham Lincoln into the Dakota language. Riggs thought that the story of Lincoln's struggles to educate himself would be a great object lessons for the students. The pamphlet that resulted was probably initially just intended for the students at the school, but re-emerged in the early 1940's to join the virtually limitless catalogue of books, etc. about Lincoln. Reverend Garvie Riggs also translated and compiled a dictionary of the Sioux language, and he translated Indian myths and legends.

We also know that Henry worked in blacksmithing and on the farm, and that he was in instrumental music. We know that instead of being forbidden to speak an Indian language, at Santee he was actually taught one. Dakota was the language spoken there. We know that he lived in Whitney Hall with 23 other boys. We know that the official school roster identified Henry not just as Henry Clarence Cloud but also as Wonaġilehunka (King of Spirit) and with his clan name. However, more importantly, we know that for the first he was exposed in a serious way to history, literature, and art. He said about Santee, "Here my soul awoke for the first time to some appreciation of the fact that there is much to learn and much to do."[7] At Santee Henry read Samuel Smiles' book *Self-Help*. He said that the book convinced him to continue his education, to work his way through school, and to stay far away from government run schools. Smiles said that, "it may be of comparatively little consequence how a man is governed from without, whilst everything depends upon how he governs himself."[8] That statement had to mean something to a young man who had grown up in a culture that emphasized self-control. It might also mean something to our world today as we daily witness "world leaders" who lack this fundamental self control. Henry went on to say that, as a result of reading the book, he resolved to "stay away from government institutions."[9] This was a resolution that unfortunately he failed to honor later in his life.

While powerful and meaningful, Henry's days at the Santee Normal and Training School were numbered. Although he was listed as being on track to graduate from the three-tiered secondary school in 1902, that day never came. He did not "return to the blanket"—an expression used to describe what happens when a student returned to the tribe before finishing school. With the support, and with the urging, of Miss E. Jean Kennedy, the matron in Whitney Hall, he applied for admission to Mount Hermon Preparatory School in Massachusetts.

Wo-Na-Xi-Lay-Hunka's date of birth might be in question, but of one thing there was no doubt—his life had changed and was still changing when he left Santee. His world stopped its slow but inevitable expansion and exploded. From 1884–1901, as was with Henry Cloud, life was a contradiction and things were changing for people all over the world.

NOTES

1. *Woonspe-Wankantu,* (Santee, Nebraska: Santee Normal Training School Press, 1901), 5.
2. "Santee Normal Training School," *The Word Carrier,* (Santee, Nebraska, November 1900), 1.
3. Ibid., 1.
4. Charles Alexander Eastman, *From the Deep Woods to Civilization,* (Mineloa: Dover Publications, 2003), 27.
5. Henry Roe Cloud, "In Memoriam: Alfred Longley Riggs," (*The American Indian Magazine,* 1916): 182.
6. Henry Roe Cloud, "From Wigwam to Pulpit," *Missionary Review of the World,* (May 1915), 12.
7. Ibid, 12.
8. Samuel Smiles, *Self Help,* (New York: American Book Company, 1904), 8.
9. Cloud, "From Wigwam to Pulpit," 12.

Chapter Five

The World outside Nebraska, 1884–1901

The good news was a series of events that brought the world together as it had never been before. Radio and telegraphs improved communication; the International Red Cross was established; the revived Olympics brought nations together in Athens; and philanthropists like Nobel and Carnegie were funding humanitarian projects. The bad news was the increasing amount of money that major nations were spending on military and weapons, in spite of international conferences to discuss limiting arms. World leaders were assassinated at an alarming rate, and the spirit of nationalism was burning in the news, and in the hearts of men and women on several continents.

Like Native Americans, indigenous peoples were living as minorities in nations controlled by others, and they felt that leaders who did not have their best interests at heart were determining their destinies. The Balkans, a region of Slavic people controlled by the Austro-Hungarian Empire, was known as "the powder keg of Europe" and within a generation would host the beginning of World War I. Irish Home Rule was rejected by the British House of Lords, and the French were expanding their influence in Indochina. Boxers in China were trying to push foreigners out, Armenians were being slaughtered in Turkey, and in South Africa the Boer Wars brought years of violence to the British, Dutch and native tribes.

The Industrial Revolution had provided the power and the ambition for nations to be on the move, literally and figuratively, and inevitably, some collided. The most powerful nations in the world carved up Africa, and it followed that in the scramble, claims would overlap, tempers would flare and Europe would come to the brink of war several times.

Industrialists had discovered Africa and Asia and all the raw materials and new markets they provided blossoming economies. British, French and German generals counted thousands of new recruits for their armies, and certain areas of distant continents offered geopolitical advantages to both large and small countries in Europe. That the natives living in those areas were not in favor of European influence did not seem to bother the industrialized nations at all. In fact, many felt it was their duty to civilize these people and convert them to Christianity for their own good- just as was the case with Native Americans. "The White Man's Burden" made it incumbent on the more advanced nations to help "backward" people, meaning those whose religion or culture differed from theirs. Echoing that same sentiment, in 1889 Indian Commissioner Thomas J. Morgan wrote that "the Indians must conform to 'the white man's way,' peaceably if they will, forcibly if they must."[1]

Railroads were built to move raw materials and finished products to market, and to move armies to protect those markets. From 1986 to 1901, four railroads characterize the drive for economic potential and national interests of the developed world: the Canadian Pacific Railroad was completed from coast to coast; the Germans were building a railroad from Berlin to Bagdad; Czar Nicholas II's Trans-Siberian Railroad reached the eastern city of Port Arthur on the Yellow Sea; and Britain's ambitious Capetown to Cairo rail system was attempted through the length of Africa. Closer to Nebraska, the Atchison, Topeka, and Sana Fe Railroad was completed. Just like Wo-Na-Xi-Lay-Hunka, subjected people all over the world heard the sounds of the ring of the axe and the crash of the falling trees as they fell before the blows struck by the hands of their own people, and these railroads took shape.

The United States did not exist in isolation from other aspects of the global movements. In 1893, Hawaii was annexed; America agreed to protect Cuba and to build a canal through Panama. As a result of the Spanish American war in 1898, the U.S. took control of Puerto Rico, the Philippine Islands, Guam, and Wake Island. The U.S. built military bases in these regions to protect American owned property and businesses, and it established schools, built roads and churches and improved sanitation. The government made it clear that it would intervene if American interests were threatened.

During this time period in Wo-Na-Xi-Lay-Hunka's/Henry Cloud's life there were several major themes that characterized change—change globally and change in his narrower world. Three of the themes that run through his story are the imperialistic behaviors of mighty nations resulting in the plight of indigenous peoples all over the world, the progressive/populist ideas of education and what all it could do, and the power of religion as a tool of assimilation. These themes would run like threads, woven together to create the cloth of the man who would become Henry Roe Cloud and the tapestry of the times in which he lived.

NOTES

1. David Eugene Wilkins, *American Indian Politics and the American Political System,* (Lanham: Rowan & Littlefield Publishers, 2006),106.

For more information on events in this chapter, consider the following sources:

David P. Forsythe, *The Humanitarians: The International Committee of the Red Cross* (Cambridge: Cambridge University Press, 2005).
David Miller, The *Official History of the Olympic Games and the IOC: From Athens to Beijing, 1894-2008* (Edinburgh: Mainstream Publishing, 2008).
Kenne Fant, *Alfred Nobel: A Biography* (New York: Arcade Publishing, 1993).
Byron Farwell, *The Great Boer War* (New York: W.W. Norton, 1990).
Steven G. Marks, *The Road to Power: Trans-Siberian Railway and the Colonization of Asian Russia, 1850-1927* (London: I. B. Tauris & Co Ltd, 1991).
Gregory Fremont-Barnes, *The Boer War, 1899-1902* (New York: Osprey, 2003).
Harmon Tupper, *To the Great Ocean: Siberia and the Trans-Siberian Railway* (London: Little,Brown and Co. 1965).
Gavan Daws, *Shoal of Time: A History of the Hawaiian Islands* (Honolulu: University of Hawaii Press, 1989).
Dr. Phil Barnes, *A Concise History of the Hawaiian Islands* (Hilo: Petroglyph Press, Ltd., 1999).

Chapter Six

Mount Hermon Preparatory School for Boys

By the early 1880's Dwight L. Moody's evangelical star had not yet started to dim. However, he increasingly began devoting more of his time and energy to endeavors that, in the long run, would be more meaningful than the revivalism for which he is so commonly known. In 1879, he started Northfield Seminary for Girls, and in 1881, he established the Mount Hermon School for Boys. Moody had been interested in starting a school for a long time. Earlier in his career, he had organized a mission Sunday school program in Chicago's East Side. He envisioned this mission as developing into a school, but with limited resources and no real influential contacts, this dream faded. By the 1880's he had access to both financial resources and influential associates, and his dream was realized. The property for the school was purchased in November of 1879 largely as a result of a gift of $25,000 from Hiram Camp, a clock- maker from New Haven, Connecticut. Moody was a present and active force at the school until his death in 1899. After that, his son William took his place.

Two sizeable farms and several smaller tracts of land were bought, and the campus ultimately occupied over 700 acres. The school officially opened for instruction on May 4, 1881. From 1881 until 1883, the school was home to 25 students. By 1899, that number had grown to over 400. When Henry Cloud enrolled in 1899, the average age of the young men there was 20.

The school catalogue explained that "the school is situated on the west side of the Connecticut River, opposite Northfield, on high sloping ground, commanding an extensive view of river valley, and mountain. The site was selected with reference to the best sanitary conditions, good drainage, pure air, excellent water; to remoteness from crowded neighborhoods; and to freedom from adverse influences often found in large villages."[1]

Chapter Six

A kind of precursor to the *U.S. News and World Report* list of best colleges entitled *Where to Educate: A Guide to the Best Private Schools, Higher Institutions of Learning, etc. in the United States, 1898–1899*, edited by Grace Powers Thomas, described Mount Hermon this way:

> Mount Hermon, Franklin County, Henry F. Cutler, B.A. Principal, was established at the suggestion of Mr. Dwight L. Moody, by several gentlemen interested in the practical Christian education of boys and young men. It was opened in May 1881, and incorporated in 1882. Mr. Hiram Cam, the late president of the board of trustees, gave $25,000, and several thousands were received from Great Britain. The school is situated on the west side of the Connecticut River, opposite the town of Northfield. The amount of land owned by the school is more than seven hundred acres. The important buildings are twelve in number. The school is designed to meet the needs of young men to whom the early opportunities of study have been denied. Applicants for admission must be at least sixteen years of age, must have good health, mental ability, and moral character. Such are received on probation without regard to their scholarship attainments. Each student is required to work two hours daily two upon the school farm, or to discharge some assigned duty about the buildings. Opportunity is given for self-help in the payment of expenses. The certificate of the principal admits to many leading colleges. The necessary expenses are about $118 per year.[2]

The school was established "for young men of sound bodies, good minds, and high aims,"[3] and although at its beginning the school was intended to provide a high quality education for students who might not otherwise been able to afford it, by the time Henry got there several young men from wealthy families had enrolled just in an effort to get better prepared for college.

The school's stated purpose also addressed the importance of the students already having determined a "serious purpose in life." "Vicious or idle boys"[4] were not welcomed or wanted. The school's Christian orientation was also made abundantly clear. A committee made up of Harvard professors came to Mount Hermon in 1894 to examine the school, and they took special note of this orientation and seemed to approve. One of the examiners commented on the "unpolished earnestness" of the faculty, that "commands respect and keeps it." Another one noted that school officials believed the religious instruction should bind the students together "into a harmonious working force and certainly that result is, in some way or other attained."[5] Charles Eastman (Ohyesia) visited the school while he was living in Boston. In reporting the following incident, he said, "During the three years I studied in Boston, I went every summer to Mr. Moody's famous summer school at Northfield, and was much interested in his strong personality. One morning as we walked together, we came to a stone at the roadside. "Eastman," said he, "this stone is a reminder of the cruelty of your countrymen two centuries ago. Here they murdered an innocent Christian."

"Mr. Moody," I replied, "it might have been better if they had killed them all. Then you would not have had to work so hard to save the souls of their descendents."[6]

Having decided to forego his last year at Santee, Henry Cloud completed his application for Mount Hermon in the late spring of 1901. He applied for admission beginning the next fall term. In his application, Henry was remarkably frank. He admitted that, to this point in his life, he had not directly supported himself. In a letter to the principal, Henry said, "Though I have had no past experience in the effort of self-support, my determination to do so, I hope, puts my inexperience out of question."[7] His life had been restricted to the reservation and to the government schools. He did not see the time he had spend in the various vocationally oriented experiences at school as being life supporting. However, Henry bluntly stated that things were going to change from this point on. Away from home and away from the government schools, the responsibility was directly his. Henry stated that his ambition in life was either to be a musician or an engineer. Then, in a statement that should certainly be well received by prep school college admission officers today, he added that he thought that there was a difference between ambition and purpose. His purpose was to serve God, and that would take precedence over his ambition. He said, "My ambition was at first, to be an engineer, and later to be a musician, Strange to say, my purpose at present is not in accord with my ambition. Santee and its training seems to be God's method of revealing to me *His Will,* with such force that I cannot but bend my will and renounce my former ambition to His Commission."[8]

Friends and mentors wrote letters of recommendation. Alfred Riggs stated that, although he was an exceptional bright young man, he was not at the same educational level with white students his age. He added that he was "better than the average Indian."[9] From the reservation school his minister, William Findley, said that "he had stood the test of his home life among his people, and that is a big thing to say." He went on to say that there were very few white boys of 18 that could "surpass him in the traits of character which we most esteem." He concluded by saying that "presumably everyone has a limit to ability. And Indians sometimes show a limit sooner than the white race, but Dr. Riggs[sic] judgment in that line is much better than mine as the lad has been under his instruction for three years last."[10] The principal of the school, Henry F. Cutler, reviewed the application and supporting letters, and he approved Henry's enrollment for the fall term. Henry Cloud was not the first Native American to attend Mount Hermon. In fact, of the first 100 students, 16 had been Indian.

When he stepped from the platform and on to the train, Henry committed himself to a series of firsts. It was the first time he had ever ridden on a train. It was the first time he had left Nebraska. He was not going off to "see some writing" with his brother, and he was not going to another boarding school with several of his friends and classmates. Having endured the soul loneliness following the death of his parents and grandmother, having experienced the isolation from his friends and culture after accepting the white man's religion, having seen all of his fellow Winnebago friends leave Santee, he was now truly alone. Even in a crowded railroad car, he was alone. Surreptitious glances and prolonged stares reinforced the fact that he was different. A cacophony of sounds, a blur of sights as they raced through the countryside, and the knowledge that he did not know and understand everything that was happening to him numbed Henry.

At one point he became convinced that his shoes, dirty and scuffed as they were, had been stolen. He verbally confronted the night porter on the train only to discover that they had been cleaned, polished, and set outside his compartment. Later, as his epic journey neared its end, he thought that he saw a group of Native Americans on the train. He rushed to them excitedly and started speaking in Winnebago. He came to find out that they were Japanese students headed for Mount Hermon as well. Henry, at a young age, was beginning to realize how much he really did not know. When he finally reached Northfield, he hurried from the train, grabbed his lone suitcase, and hurried off toward the school. Perhaps he was embarrassed and self-conscious; perhaps he felt isolated; perhaps he simply wanted to be by himself at this pivotal moment. Regardless, he deliberately separated himself from the other students, their laughter, and their frivolity.

When he arrived at Mount Hermon, Henry had $100. He had concealed it in his undershirt because he had been told by his friends in Winnebago that unscrupulous whites would try to take advantage of him. He had earned the money by working, and some of it was a portion of his annuity. He had enough money for two terms at the school. Finally, he was there, and he had committed himself to that road about which his grandmother had cautioned him.

Although by Genoa, reservation school, and Santee standards, Henry was an outstanding student, this was different. He was not prepared to deal with the academic challenges he would face at this college preparatory school. New students were required to take entrance examinations on the first day of the new school term. They were given in arithmetic, grammar, geography, United States History, spelling, writing, elementary English, and Bible. Having passed these courses in other schools was not accepted as evidence of competency. Students who did not pass these examinations were not sent home, but they were required to enroll in what was called the Preparatory Department. Henry passed only the tests in Bible, writing (penmanship), spelling, and geography. The rest of his academic course load was preparatory. The school catalog contained sample questions from the entrance examination. These are some examples from the sections he failed.

Mathematics

What is the unit of length in the metric system? How are the units of weight and captivity derived from it? What is the weight in kilograms of a cube of water whose edges are 5.7 centimeters in length?

A manufactory uses 24 tons of coal a day, 20% of which is lost in smoke. How much coal would be needed if this waste could be prevented?

A four months note for $5000, dated January 10, 1901, and bearing 7% interest was discounted at a bank on March 15, at 6%. Find the proceeds. (No days of grace.)

English

Write sentences to illustrate:
Attribute (or subjective) complement
Infinitive phrase used as a subject.
Appositive (explanatory modifier).
Indirect object
Adverb clause of time
Give the construction of the italicized words and phrases below:
"Blow, blow, *thou* winter *wind*,
Thou art not so unkind
As *man's* ingratitude."
They ran *to call* him and give him the ticket.
"The quality *of mercy* is not strained;
It droppeth *as* the gentle rain from heaven
Upon the place beneath."
Correct, giving reasons for each change:
Each person will provide their own lunch.
He don't look so very tall.
Can we go over to the river?

Composition

Write a business letter to apply for a situation.

Write an essay of at least two hundred and fifty words on one of the following; be careful to divide it into proper paragraphs:
The Old Schoolhouse
My Room
An Unexpected Swim
The Complaint of the Blackboard
How I Broke My Colt

What Trusts Are
My Favorite Books

U.S. History
Name three French, three Spanish and three English explorers, and tell what each did.
Describe Burgoyne's Campaign.
Give a complete account of Benedict Arnold.[11]

While it is obvious that the exam was not easy, is was true that, despite his intelligence, determination, and character, Henry was a victim of a governmental philosophy that regarded the education of Native Americans as almost exclusively assimilation and vocational training. Even with the additional support of the preparatory program, he failed algebra and had to retake the final examination. However, he did eventually prove to be a very good student and soon was able to enroll in the regular program and classes.

Mount Hermon had an exceptionally detailed and explicit school catalogue. The same man, Henry F. Cutler, was principal of the school for 42 years from 1890–1932. Consequently, there is good documentation of the type of coursework and extra-curricular activities in which Henry participated. For example, by looking at the commencement program for 1902 we see that he shared the third place prize for the outstanding preparatory student with two other classmates.[12] Henry Clarence Cloud soon distinguished himself within his class and the school.

One of the most telling things about the time Henry spent at Mount Hermon is revealed in the fact that he when he completed his preparation/remediation he selected the "classical course" of study. That program was designed "to furnish adequate preparation for admission to academic courses in any college. The aim of the course is to train the pupil to exact methods of thought and to accurate expression not only in Greek and Latin, but in English. With this in view much attention is paid to the study of English in connection with ancient languages."[13] Clearly, students in this program of study were looking forward to enrolling in prestigious colleges. Other programs included the Latin Scientific Course for those who wanted to enter scientific study or practice but who also wanted to go to colleges with a classical orientation and required Latin, French, or German; and the Scientific Course, which prepared students for scientific or technical schools not requiring those foreign languages. The Elective Course was offered for students who needed some greater degree of freedom in course selection than the others afforded. By selecting the Classical Course, Henry symbolically separated himself as far as he could from the government school and its philosophy, He had determined to never attend another government school, and there was certainly no way to confuse his current program of study with one. On a more practical level, he had confirmed his dedication to a purpose rather than to an ambition.

There was more to life at Mount Hermon than just academics. Henry participated in a number of different activities and was apparently good at what he did. He was named to the All Hermon football and baseball teams. His athletic interests were far ranging—he played polo one year as well. Henry was also a member of the Good Government Club. In 1906 he was Salutatorian and class president, and no doubt led his classmates in the class yell.

>   Zoo-ke —Ku-zum —Ka-rax—Ka-rix
>   Zoo-ke —Ku-zum —Ka-rax—Ka-rix
>   Ki-li—Ki-leben—Ki-Inn—Ki—lix
>   Hermon—Hermon—Nineteen Six[14]

The Young Men's Christian Association (Y.M.C.A.) was particularly active on the Mount Hermon campus. Dwight L. Moody had been the president of the Chicago Y.M.C.A. was adamant about bringing the association to Mount Hermon. In fact, the school hosted an annual Y.M.C.A. summer conference for intercollegiate branches. The school catalogue reported that Mount Hermon had sent delegates to the various conventions of the College Y.M.C.A., and through this organization, Mount Hermon was affiliated with different schools and colleges throughout the land. "It's (YMCA) membership averages at least three fourths of all of the students."[15] Henry participated in the organization by playing in the Y.M.C.A. Orchestra and held district leadership positions.

During the time he was there, debate also flourished at Mount Hermon. By the time he left there were five different literary and debate societies. A 1905 article reported that the Good Government Club and the Philomathean Society had a debate on the topic "The Advantages of Labor Unions to the Laboring Man." Although it was described as an "able and close contest," the Philomathean Society won the debate.[16]

Mount Hermon also hosted numerous distinguished speakers and guests. Professor William North Rice from Wesleyan visited the school to talk about "Tennyson the Poet of Science." In 1902, Charles A. Eastman visited Mount Hermon and spoke to the students there, and In September of that ear, arguably the most famous visitor—President Theodore Roosevelt came to the school. The school newspaper, *The Hermonite,* reported it this way.

> At 5:45 o'clock in the afternoon of September 1, Labor Day, the train pulled into the little station which was hardly recognizable in its garb of color, and Mr. Roosevelt stepped from his car and was formally received by Messrs. W.R., Paul, and A.G. Moody with Dr. Pentecost and the selectmen of Northfield,

who escorted him to the carriage, in which he was rapidly driven to the Chapel.

The farmer folk had come from far and near, for to most of them this was the opportunity of a lifetime, not to be missed under any circumstances, and the campus was literally thronged with vehicles of all descriptions, gaudily decked out for the most with flags and bunting which flapped gaily in the breeze, and in company with the decorations which were displayed on the various halls and cottages of the School gave one the impression of the Fourth of July rather than a cool day in September.

The first sight of "Teddy" was the signal for everyone in the house to rise to his feet and "yell" and after a moment or so of individual work along this line, the fellows gave the regular School "yell" with "Roosevelt" on the end, which seemed to tickle the Chief Executive immensely for his face wore a very substantial smile as he bowed his acknowledgements.[17]

In *From Wigwam to Pulpit,* Henry Cloud talked about the drudgery of having to study, and like many students he did not always see the use of much of what he was studying. He admitted that he simply did not have the background nor had he acquired the study skills to make it anything but drudgery. He worked on his conjugations and translations by tacking cards to the plow as he worked in the fields. He often did not get as much plowed as the farmer he was working for had wanted.

Like many college students, his financial situation was never solid. There are several letters to the school from Henry and others dealing with these concerns. In February, 1903 Miss Dora B. Dodge, who identified herself as a former teacher at Santee, wrote Dr. Cutler offering her assistance, "He (Henry) has been somewhat discouraged because of lack of funds. I have written that with Mrs. Dr. Wolf's help, I would see that his bills were paid."[18]

Proceedings from the Mohonk Indian Conference in 1896 indicate that Miss Dodge was considerably more than just a former teacher. The treasurer of that conference, Mr. Frank Woods, writing about the closing of the Oahe Mission in South Dakota, said of her, "The thought of that missionary, Miss Dora B. Dodge, has haunted me ever since. She is a capable, earnest, refined, cultivated woman, fitted to grace any sphere in society; but, with rare consecration, she has separated herself from nearly everything that constitutes life for us, and has buried herself in the midst of the densest savagery, ninety miles from the nearest town, Bismarck, where she frequently has to wait several weeks for her mails, and is sometimes months without seeing a white face. And she does this for the love of Christ and the despised red man, these pagans in a Christian land, whom He died to save. How will she feel when she hears that this mission is to be given up?"[19] Henry was fortunate to have such advocates.

Eventually in 1904, he had to take an entire year off to get enough money to continue at the school. He wrote to Dr. Cutler, "Matters have developed in such a way as to compel me to make a decided change in my plans. I have decided to stay out of Hermon on year."[20] He worked on a farm in New Jersey. Elizabeth DuBois, a member of a church near the farm wrote Dr. Cutler asking if he thought that Henry was "worthy of help."[21] Apparently, Henry had approached her Sunday School class for assistance. The farm was the site of a Revolution War battle, and Cloud was constantly digging up cannon balls and other war relics as he plowed. He was very enterprising and created a little museum by lining these relics up on the farmer's porch for tourists to see. In perhaps one of the most telling comments in his autobiography, he talks about these trying days, "During these five years I learned to pay for what I got, and by actual struggle, came to know the value of a dollar, and the meaning of toil, and something of the worth of time."[22]

Henry's interests were changing and becoming more focused. He talked about the "brighter side" of life that consisted of reading *The Old Tennent Church* and *The Journals of David Brainerd*. Frank R. Symmes, the church's fifteenth pastor, compiled *The History of the Old Tennent Church* in 1904. Symmes described the heritage and importance of the church, which was now named the First Presbyterian Church of the County of Monmouth (New Jersey).

> This sanctuary, now widely known as Old Tennent, is a relic and a witness, a land-mark and a monument. It is a treasured heritage from stern and sturdy servants of God transmitted to their descendents through a number of generations, testifying to the history of a rugged faith in the eternal word of the Lord and of a noble and steadfast adherence to principle. This house is the proof positive of the sacred past speaking to the observing present. That splendid profound document, the Declaration of Independence, a parchment carefully preserved under glass is fading in its ink, and possibly will soon need to be deposited in a dark case to preserve the clear, strong chirography of its precious pages; but Old Tennent edifice was standing twenty-five years before the Declaration was written, and through all the years since has stood exposed to the weather of storm and sun and wind, straight and strong to-day, and good for many years more if with God's providence her children will love her with faithful care.[23]

The book went on to detail such things as sketches of its pastors, biographical references to its members, all of its earlier record lists, full quotations of its earlier historical records, a complete list of burials in all of its graveyards, many of its local traditions, most of its important illustrations and maps, an account of the battle of Monmouth, and a large collection of genealogical notes. It is hard to see how a young man could find this epic either interesting or "bright." On the other hand, *The Journal of David Brainerd*, seems to be the very type of book he would find compelling.

Edited by Jonathan Edwards, who delivered the famous *Sinners in the Hands of an Angry God* sermon, this journal has inspired and invigorated missionaries all over the world.[24] David Brainerd was one of nine children born into a devoutly Puritan family in Connecticut in 1718. His father died when he was nine years old. Five years later, his mother died. David lived with his older sister until he was nineteen. He tried farming but realized that his heart was simply not in that endeavor. He turned to studying the Bible with Phineas Fiske, a minister. During his studies he frequently tried fasting as a way of gaining a clearer understanding of God's word and intent. During his conversion, he felt an "unspeakable glory." He enrolled at Yale and was preparing for the ministry when he was diagnosed with tuberculosis. In 1742, David was expelled from Yale for refusing to apologize or "confess" to saying that one of his tutors had "no more grace than his chair." He lapsed into a period of depression and melancholy that plagued him for the rest of his short life. Edwards carefully edited the journals to remove any references that might reflect poorly on him. Brainerd found his calling when he began ministering to the Native Americans. He became a full-time missionary to the Indians. He was driven in his pursuits. He walked hundreds of miles through extremes in weather. He taught them, he cared for them, he prayed for and with them, and he suffered with them. His emotional health with his extreme highs and lows was complicated by a reoccurrence of tuberculosis. He died in 1747. Brainerd's extraordinary life story was a source of motivation for Henry Cloud.

During his time away from Mount Hermon, Henry wrote an article for the Santee Normal Training School newspaper *The Word Carrier* about his experiences in New Jersey. In that article he indicated that he had been asked to write about his "life purpose and (his) present work." He described the Battle Ground Farm, its related history, and the virtues of being able to plow a straight furrow. He talked about Brainard, his missionary work among the Indians, the Old Tennent Church, and the reverence he felt when he thought about the Indians who had participated in worship and communion there years before. A large portion of the letter was a validation of the time he had spent at Santee. He praised the "curriculum, of studies and course of manual training suited to our needs. She is able to equip us with education of head and heart to be men and women of solid worth wherever our lost may be cast." He praised the missionary teachers at Santee and their "superlative kindness." He said that "Santee has taken the infant life of an Indian race, and with the gospel food is nourishing it," and he concluded by saying that "I am striving to be a missionary. Whether I be a minister, a medical missionary, a layman, or a Christian farmer it is to God's glory."[25]

There were many unanswered questions for Henry Cloud as he finished Mount Hermon, but his broad interpretation of his "life-purpose" was become clearer. The mention of these two books, *The Journal of David Brainerd* and *The History of the Old Tennent Church* in *From Wigwam to Pulpit* and in this newspaper article is not incidental. Cloud's affinity to the Presbyterian Church had grown and would eventually manifest itself in ordination into the ministry. His next educational destination was soon to be determined as well. By any measure, his time in Northfield was successful. In his last year there, he was elected president of his class and delivered the salutatory address at commencement, and in 1906, after five years at Mount Hermon, Henry Clarence Cloud was ready for college. He would start this new stage in his life with the beginnings of an educational philosophy and with a maturing set of religious convictions. These three strands—education, religion, and service to "his people"—formed the fabric of the man who has been called the "latter day father of the Indian nations."[26]

Much like Charles Eastman, Henry Cloud equated a good college education with schools in New England. He had visited the campuses at Yale, Princeton, and Wesleyan but was planning to attend Dartmouth College in Hanover, New Hampshire primarily because of their commitment to the education of Indians. However, acting on a challenge from a classmate, Henry took the Yale Prelims and passed eight of the fourteen exams. He then decided to attend Yale.

NOTES

1. "Catalogue," *Catalogue of Mount Hermon School,* (Mount Hermon: Press of E.L. Hildreth and Co. 1898), 18.

2. Grace Powers Thomas, *Where to Educate: A Guide to the Best Private Schools, Higher Institutions, etc. in the United States,* (Boston: Brown and Company Publishers, 1898), 160.

3. "Catalogue," *Catalogue of Mount Hermon School,* (Mount Hermon: Press of E.L. Hildreth and Co. 1898), 18.

4. Ibid., 18—19.

5. James Findlay, "Education and Church Controversy: The Later Career of Dwight L. Moody," (*The New England Quarterly, Vol. 39, No. 2,* June 1966): 212

6. Charles Alexander Eastman, *From the Deep Woods to Civilization,* (Mineloa: Dover Publications, 2003), 43.

7. Henry C. Cloud to Henry F. Cutler, Santee, Nebraska, 28 May 1901, Northfield Mount Hermon School Archives, Mount Hermon, Massachusetts.

8. Ibid.

9. A.L. Riggs to Henry F. Cutler, Santee, Nebraska, 7 June 1901, Northfield Mount Hermon School Archives, Mount Hermon, Massachusetts.

10. William to Henry F. Cutler, Winnebago, Nebraska, 16 June 1901, Northfield Mount Hermon School, Mount Hermon Archives, Massachusetts.

11. "Catalogue." *Catalogue of Mount Hermon School,* (Mount Hermon: Press of E.L. Hildreth and Co. 1898), 99.

12. "Catalogue," *Catalogue of Mount Hermon School,* (Mount Hermon: Press of E.L. Hildreth and Co. 1902), 82.

13. "Catalogue," *Catalogue of Mount Hermon School,* (Mount Hermon: Press of E.L. Hildreth and Co. 1898), 36.

14. Class Day Program, 1906, Northfield Mount Hermon School, Mount Hermon Archives, Massachusetts.

15. Catalogue," *Catalogue of Mount Hermon School,* (Mount Hermon: Press of E.L. Hildreth and Co. 1906), 38.

16. "Mount Hermon," *Record of Christian Work*, 1905, 246.

17. "The President's Visit to Mount Hermon," *The Hermonite* (Mount Hermon School, 20 September 1902), 1 -2.

18. Dora Dodge to Henry F. Cutler, Brooklyn, New York, 1 February 1903, Northfield Mount Hermon School Archives, Mount Hermon, Massachusetts.

19. Frank Woods, "Second Session," *Proceedings of the 13th Annual Lake Mohonk Conference of Friends of the Indian,* (The Lake Mohonk Conference, 1896), 104.

20. Henry C. Cloud to Henry F. Cutler, Freehold, New Jersey,10 August 1904, Northfield Mount Hermon School Archives, Mount Hermon, Massachusetts.

21. Elizabeth DuBois to Henry F. Cutler, Tennent, New Jersey,31 October 1904, Northfield Mount Hermon School Archives, Mount Hermon, Massachusetts.

22. Henry Roe Cloud, "From Wigwam to Pulpit," *Missionary Review of the World*, (May 1915), 13.

23. Henry Cloud, "Henry Cloud and Tennent Church." *The Word Carrier,*Santee Normal Training School, May—June 1905.

24. Frank R.Symmes, *The History of the Old Tennent Church,* (Cranbury: George W. Burroughs, 1904), 7.

25. Henry Cloud, "Henry Cloud and Tennent Church," *The Word Carrier,* Santee: Santee Normal Training school, May—June 1905.

26. Thomas Sorci, "Latter Day Father of the Indian Nations," *The News* 27, no. 3, (Summer 1988).

Chapter Seven

Yale

Henry Cloud entered Yale in 1906, and it was not long before he came to realize exactly what that meant. In *From Wigwam to Pulpit,* he wrote, "As I lay on my couch in Pierson Hall, the singing of the approaching Sophomores grew louder and louder. Soon they filled my room, and things happened to me that only a Yale man knows. After the ordeal was over I was a Yale man. It was a great moment for me when, marching through the streets, I joined with several thousand students for the first time in the cry of Aristophanes' frogs."[1] We know that the words of "Wake, Freshman, Wake," the song the sophomores were singing, gives some subtle forewarning for the newbies at Yale.

> The stars brightly glancing
> Behold us advancing,
> And kindly smile upon us from on high;
> Our summons awaiting,
> With hearts loudly beating,
> The Freshmen trembling on their couches lie.[2]

In 1899, Lewis Sheldon in *Yale: Her Campus, Class-rooms, and Athletics,* addressed the issue of how freshmen went about becoming real Yale men. He described how, when he was a student at Yale, the freshmen and sophomores met in what he called "a truly glorious strife." Locked in a tight formation he described as the "most perfect sardine formation," the students held tightly to each other en mass, and the freshmen and sophomores rushed toward each other—assuming that an amoebic mob of hundreds of students clutching each other and who had to step forward or back at the same time in order to move at all can rush. Welch saw that extreme closeness as being symbolic of the spiritual and physical unity that was a result of the process. He observed that, "As individuals we were fond of many of them, but as a class we truly despised them."[3] After the collision, the student was made to feel that he was finally part of the class and part of Yale.

The excitement has far from being over. From the class rush, the students moved on to the fence rush. The rules of this ritual were simple. Freshmen would gather in front of the Grammar School and then try walk two or three abreast down the street for about one block to Elm Street. A fence was beside the sidewalk. If, by chance, some wayward group of sophomore should lie upon them, and they always did, the freshmen would grab and hold on to the fence until the sophomores dislodged them or the fence gave way.

Whether or not he agreed with Welch's depiction of these events as a "glorious struggle," Henry Cloud clearly bought into the idea of the Yale man. If he ever felt intimidated or self-conscious, it was not apparent to anyone at Yale. He became just as immersed in campus activities, was just as well-known and popular, and was just as outspoken and adamant about his goals as he was in Northfield. Despite being a Yale man, many of the problems that had haunted him throughout his life away from Winnebago continued to do so. He still had on-going and serious problems with expenses, and despite being well-known and achieving moderate academic success, he still saw himself at a disadvantage because the other Yale men were from wealthy families, higher social status, and had better and more complete educations than he had. Regardless, on that first night at Yale, as he roamed the streets of New Haven with other Yale men announcing both their literal and figurative arrival like Aristophanes' frogs—"Brekekekex, brekekekex, ko-ax, ko-ax," Henry Clarence Cloud felt that he was in the right place.

The vocational courses at government schools surely seemed far removed from the rigors of academic life at Yale. Henry was now taking courses in Yale's Academical Department that not only focused on languages and philosophy, which he favored, but also on math and science, which he endured. Although he was fairly disciplined about preparing for his classes, Henry certainly did not lock himself in his room or sequester himself in the library and do nothing but study. He was highly visible around campus, and everyone apparently liked him, or at least he intrigued them. His years at Yale are well documented, and the novelty of having a real Indian as a student did not go unnoticed. *The New Haven Daily-Journal* proclaimed Henry one of the three most interesting students at Yale—the other two were Cheng-t-ing from Ningpo, China and Robert A. Taft, Jr., the President's son. Taft was a teammate of Henry's on the debate team. Henry seemed to try to sample some of the best that college life had to offer. He played intramurals, contributed to the literary magazine, and attended all of the games a Yale man was expected to attend.

While he was a student at Yale, he joined a fraternity. Beta Theta Pi, his fraternity of choice, was founded in 1839. Interestingly, and perhaps in some way appealing to this native westerner, Beta Theta Pi was the first fraternity founded west of the Allegheny Mountains and the first to locate a chapter west of the Mississippi River. The Yale chapter, Phi Chi, was founded in 1892. In more recent years the Yale chapter has fallen on some difficult times. It was not operating from 1968 until 1990, and it lost its charter again in 2007 after a fraternity member fired a handgun in the fraternity house and had apparently had stockpiled several other weapons in his room. When Henry joined the Phi Chi chapter, Beta Theta Pi's nationwide membership was close to 18,000. Its catalogue proudly says that "the badge of the fraternity is well known—its colors are pink and blue. Its flower is the rose."[4] Henry does not mention his fraternity, its well-known badge, nor its unusual choice of colors in *From Wigwam to Pulpit*. The fraternity does not mention Henry Cloud on its list of "Beta Greats." He is listed on page 976 of the Beta Theta Phi Catalogue (1917 edition) as a Presbyterian clergyman and head of Roe Indian Institute in Wichita, Kansas.[5] It is possible that Henry joined the fraternity just to become part of a group—although he was part of several different groups at Yale. It has been suggested that "fraternities recall frontier days in that they act as a substitute for the families one has left."[6] Perhaps it was the ritual or the secrets that evoked memories of the medicine lodge. It might have been none of these. Regardless, it appears that the fraternity aspect of being a Yale man had little definable impact on Cloud.

Henry was also a member of Elihu, a secret society that was named after Elihu Yale the university's primary benefactors and namesake. Elihu was founded at the university in 1903, and because it was and remains "secret" not much is known about it by those outside its membership. In one of its few public documents it says that the purposes of Elihu are "to foster among its members, by earnest work and good fellowship a stronger affection for Yale; a broader view of undergraduate life and its aims; a deeper and more helpful friendship for one another; and to give its members, after graduation, an additional tie to bind them to Yale and to each other."[7] Some accounts indicate that Henry Cloud was the first member of an ethnic minority to be "tapped" into membership of a secret society at Yale. Elihu has never actually considered itself a secret society, and a *New York Times* article about its creation tends to support that claim. "An announcement of interest to the great body of Yale graduates, detailing the foundation of a new senior class organization in the college was made to-day. A feature about it is that it is an open club and not a secret society."[8] However, just about everyone else considered it to be one of Yale's secret societies, and it has practiced a code of secrecy since its creation.

Another organization that Henry Cloud joined at Yale was the Cosmopolitan Club. In the early twentieth century, the word "cosmopolitan" and indeed the cosmopolitan movement had nothing to do with the magazine we know today. In *Life at Yale* it is stated that a "chapter of the Cosmopolitan Club, which exists in all the larger American universities, is composed of foreign students of all nationalities and native Americans whose interests are sufficiently catholic to find profit in meeting with them once a month."[9] With the motto "Above All Nations is Humanity," this organization was not extremely active politically but did seek to inform and involve college students about foreign affairs. Henry Cloud was quickly drawn to this fledging organization on the Yale campus. Growing from its origination at the first convention of the Association of Cosmopolitan Clubs at Madison, Wisconsin in 1907, it had a national membership of over 2000 by the time Cloud graduated from Yale. The Cosmopolitan Club sponsored international nights and had as its goals both providing support for international students while they were at Yale and working to increase the worldview of undergraduates there. Frank A. Fetter, in an address at the Cosmopolitan Club on June 2, 1906 spoke out passionately against the sins of imperialism and spoke to ideals that Henry Cloud could relate to by saying that "slowly have men outgrown the petty prejudices of language and race. The word foreign has never been synonymous with barbarous, outlandish, and hostile. Only slowly does each come to see beneath these superficial signs the worth and charm of a universal human nature. Then at last cosmopolitanism becomes a possibility."[10] Henry's worldview and his awareness of the plight of indigenous people in other parts of the world had been heightened. However, at the same time, he was about to embark on experiences that redirected his concern toward his native people.

Henry's greatest commitment was to the numerous religious and Bible study societies that preferred to have people describe them as secret. One religious group that he did frequently refer to by name and to which he devoted a great deal of time was the Young Men's Christian Association. Much like in the case of Charles Eastman, the Y.M.C.A. was an important part of Henry's life.

Henry Cloud graduated from Yale with nearly a B average. He was a member of numerous clubs, a fraternity, and several secret societies. He received honors for his junior dissertation. His classmates selected him the most outstanding male student. However, the single most important event during his years at Yale took place in his freshman year. One Sunday afternoon, at the Young Men's Christian Association meeting, he heard Mary Roe, the wife of Walter C. Roe, talk about Christian Indians.

NOTES

1. Henry Roe Cloud, "From Wigwam to Pulpit," *Missionary Review of the World*, (May 1915), 13.
2. Association of Yale Alumni, "the Songs," http://alumninet.yale.edu/classes/yc1961/songs.htm, Accessed 14 July 2009.
3. Lewis Sheldon Welch and Walter Camp, *Yale: Her Campus, Class-rooms, and Athletics,* (Boston: L.C. Page and Company, 1899), 5.
4. James T. Brown,*Catalogue of Beta Theta Pi, ed.* (New York: James T. Brown, 1917), viii.
5. Ibid., 976.
6. Hank Nuwer, *Wrongs of Passage: Fraternities, Sororities, Hazing, and Binge Drinking,* (Bloomington: University of Indiana Press, 2002), 117.
7. Elihu Society, http://www.elihu.org/, Accessed 14 July 2009.
8. "New Yale Senior Club," *New York Times*, (March 21, 1903), 7.
9. Edwin Rogers Embree, *Life at Yale,*ed. (New Haven: Yale University Press , 1912), 24.
10. Frank Fetter, "Imperialism and Cosmopolitanism," *The Cosmopolitan Annual*, (Ithica: Cornell University, 1907), 28.

Chapter Eight

The Roes

It was not that she was shy and retiring or that she lived in the shadow of her husband Walter Roe, the famous missionary among the Indians—far from it. It was just that Mary Roe had never had the occasion to express herself in large gatherings that much. But that changed. In November of 1898 Walter Roe had addressed attendees at a conference at Lake Mohonk not far from Poughkeepsie, New York. The evening after he spoke he and Mary were guests of Albert Smiley, the organizer of the conference, for dinner. Smiley was so impressed with Mary's passion and eloquence as she talked about the needs of Indians that he impetuously said that she needed to talk to the entire conference. Almost as she demurred, he arranged for a change of the program and scheduled her a time to speak. Her sister, Elizabeth Page reported that

> She touched on the need of the people of an opportunity for self- support, especially of the women whom the Government farming could not reach; she spoke of upholding the returned students who have had careful training but who were especially isolated in the camps, and of supplying some substitute for the old social life with its admixture of paganism, which civilization and Christianity were combining to destroy. Then she told them of her plans for building a house on the Indian reservation—such a house as would not be beyond the reach of any ambitious family.[1]

As a result of her short, five minute speech a star was born in the missionary field and among humanitarians concerned about the Indians. On a more tangible level, she raised over $1,200 to build the house she described. The following year the house, dubbed the Mohonk Lodge, was built, and Mary Roe emerged as a prominent figure in missionary work. She remained that way for the rest of her life.

Walter and Mary Roe were noteworthy in their own right. Both were well-educated. Walter was from an established family in the East, and so was Mary. That was the problem—they were from the same family. Walter Clark Roe, the second son of James Gilbert and Caroline Clark Roe, was born in 1859. He graduated from Williams College in 1881. After graduating he taught at the Brooklyn Polytechnic Institute and, in 1884, he joined the faculty of the Hill School in Pottstown, Pennsylvania. He remained there until he was stricken with tuberculosis in 1889. Mary Wickham was daughter of Alfred Cox Roe and Emma Wickham Roe. She was born in 1863. She received much of her education at the various schools he father established in his eclectic career such as the Cornwall Collegiate Institute for Young Ladies, the Berkeley Institute in Brooklyn, and the New York Collegiate Institute of Harlem. In 1883 she became a teacher at the New York Normal School, now Hunter College, and in 1885 joined her first cousin and future husband, Walter Clark Roe, at the Hill School. They were married in 1887 after a courtship that was marked with considerable angst and guilt. In an 1884 letter, Mary described her conflicting feelings and reportedly suggested that they return to a more friend-like relationship. There is reason to believe that, as their marriage went on, their relationship became more platonic and based on respect rather than love. Their one child, a son, died in infancy while they were at the Hill School.

Later the Roes moved to Ft. Worth, Texas, and Walter prepared for the ministry while he was convalescing. He was ordained by the southern branch of the Presbyterian Church in 1892, and he served four mission stations in the Ft. Worth area before being called to a Dallas church. During this time Mary taught at the Ft. Worth High School. It was there where they began missionary work among the Indians in earnest.

The work of the Roes with the Indians had started a couple of years before the conference at Mohonk. The women of the Board of Domestic Missions of the Reformed Church had identified Frank Hall Wright as the person to spearhead its work among the natives in the Indian Territory. He was the son of Allen Wright, a Choctaw, who had received his education at Union Theological Seminary in New York and Harriet Mitchell Wright. Mrs. Wright was a descendant of William Brewster one of the passengers on the Mayflower. Frank Wright literally followed in his father's footsteps not only in becoming a minister but he also received his education at the same schools as his father. He was described as a man with "a glorious voice, a magnetic personality and unbounded enthusiasm."[2] He had already done some unsuccessful missionary work in the Indian Territory and had returned to New York to do itinerant evangelism. In 1894, Wright was sick, weak, and apparently near death. He was suffering from tuberculosis. However, despite his health and despite the fact that he had already given up working with the Indians once, he readily accepted the charge. In 1895 he started west.

His family set up residence in Dallas, Texas, and he moved on to the Indian Territory—Oklahoma. His initial work was neither successful nor rewarding with either the Comanche or the Apache. He eventually settled some seventy miles from Fort Gill at a settlement called Colony. John Segar, the Indian agent there, invited him to stay, and Wright began his work among the Cheyenne and Arapahoe who lived in the area.

Because of his health, Wright frequently left Colony during the coldest winter months and returned to Dallas. In Dallas, he met and became friends with Walter Roe, now a Presbyterian minister, and his wife, Mary. The Roes joined Wright at the dedication of the Columbian Memorial Church in Colony. The church was named in commemoration of a tea the Women's Mission Board had on Columbus Day in New York in 1892. They raised the money for the construction of the church at that event.

Wright approached the Roes about helping him in his work at Colony. Walter Roe's health had grown progressively worse, and his doctors suggested that the open air might be good for him. Mary agreed. The Roes moved to Colony and began their work there in 1897. It was not long before Walter Roe became the resident pastor there. Reverend Wright enthusiastically renewed his traveling evangelism and was frequently gone. Walter's health continued to worsen, and the man the Indians called Iron Eyes was described as "a bespectacled little man who parted his hair in the middle and plastered it down."[3]

Walter suffered from reoccurring bouts of typhoid fever that left him bedridden for long periods of time. However, even in his weakened state he was obviously fiery and effective. Membership at the church grew rapidly. While there is not much evidence of religious instruction as such, there is a great deal of evidence that religious discipline was exercised. There were many cases of consistory hearings, and almost weekly members were confronted with charges of drunkenness, gambling, immorality, excessive absence from church, and getting marrying according to Indian customs rather than through the church.

One of the major challenges the Roes faced was that of language. The Cheyenne and Arapaho spoke different languages. Interpreters were at best inconsistent. To be effective the sermons depended on accuracy as well as the more subtle meanings and figures of speech found in the scriptures. Initially Wright set out to master Cheyenne, and the Roes determined to learn Arapaho. Wright's frequent absences complicated the matter, as did the need for immediacy. The missionaries then decided that learning the language was taking too long and was even promoting jealousy between the two tribes when it seemed like one language was being used more than the other. They tried to use a more commonly understood sign language but found it to be too limiting. They returned to using interpreters. It might seem that the missionaries were ethnocentric or even condescending by not trying to master the native tongue of their parishioners and potential converts, but it must be emphasized that the failed efforts of missionaries and educators who preceded them were often the result of efforts to completely eliminate those same native tongues.

In 1902, the Roes took a one year leave of absence to go to Europe in hopes that Walter's health might improve. On their way back they stopped in Chicago to visit Dr. Hall, a renowned eye doctor. They told him about the very large number of Indians who suffered from a variety of eye and vision problems, including what they thought was a disproportionate number who were completely blind and urged him to visit Colony. The doctor, who was well known for his very large and still growing patient load remarked that "perhaps I shall come some day when business is slack. I am sure I would like to."[4] He did.

Mary Roe said that it was a marvel to see the doctor work. Runners went out to the different settlements and camps telling them about the doctor. People who needed attention were soon being brought in to see Dr. Hall. Mary told about one old, blind Indian whose name was Cheyenne Chief—although he was an Arapaho, "He said, 'Medicine Chief, I have been praying, praying, for just a little light, not full sight, but just a little, so I can find my way to church. I want to see the faces of all these people who have given me the Jesus road. I have prayed and Jesus has sent you to us, and I ask you to take pity on me, and give me just a little light. I have been blind for many colds, and I am old, so all I ask is only a little light'."[5]

This story about the old, blind Indian was one that Mary Roe told during her speech at Yale in 1906. It made a deep impression on Henry Cloud as he sat in the audience. Writing to her after he had made a speech in the same Y.M.C.A. meeting room, he said, "I led the meeting and all the time the platform at which I stood seemed sacred to me for it was there you stood and spoke of the blind Indian chief whom the children loved so because he was a Christian."[6]

After the meeting, Professor Henry Wright, who many thought was the moral compass of Yale at that time, introduced Henry Cloud to Mrs. Roe. Cloud was both inspired and frustrated with as she talked about the increasing number of Christian Indians. Elizabeth Page, Mary's sister, quotes him as saying, "I was glad to hear you speak. I had almost begun to believe that it was impossible to Christianize the American Indian." Mrs. Roe responded, "Why, Mr. Cloud, what made you lean toward such an opinion as that?" To which he replied, "Because I am one of them."[7]

Then their conversation took an unusual but fortuitous turn. Henry had heard from people back home in Nebraska that Christian had made some inroads among the Winnebago but in a questionable form. Albert Hensley, a young Winnebago who had been educated at Carlisle, had returned home and had gained enough followers to challenge the power and mystic of the Medicine Lodge. Hensley's religion combined elements of Christianity with the use of peyote. Peyote use among the Winnebago had been around for several years primarily because of the proselytizing of John Rave. Rave praised peyote as being curative as well as producing visions. It was a simple and uncomplicated leap for traditional Winnebago to embrace the use of peyote. Their traditional religion valued fasting as a way of producing life-changing visions, and the Earthmaker had liberally placed medicinal plants and other sacred objects around for their use.

This new religion immediately caught Henry's attention. He was intimately aware of the hold the Medicine Lodge had on the Winnebago. For something or someone to successfully challenge that power was impressive. He had also witnessed the exhaustive but seemingly futile attempts of his former teachers and mentors like Findley and Riggs. While not embracing the use of peyote, Henry did recognize that Hensley's followers were rejecting their traditional, and as he frequently referred to it, paganistic teachings and were open to the teachings of Christ as revealed in the Bible. Hensley himself said, "The Holy Spirit shall be in you, and you drink this mescal and it is in you, and it brings all things to your remembrance just as Jesus said it would."[8] They were especially intrigued with the accounts found in Revelation.

Certainly Henry was wrestling with how to, or whether to try to, reconcile the peyote use with Christianity when he heard Mary Roe talk. He had almost been to the point of thinking that the Winnebago immersion in the Medicine Lodge would always prevent large numbers of Winnebago from converting to Christianity. The peyote users were at least calling on their followers to live cleaner lives and they were increasingly receptive to preaching and teaching. Mary urged him to visit them in Colony where he could see firsthand not just large numbers of Christian converts but also people whose lives had been ruined by years of use and addiction to peyote. The Roes had already tried to deal with peyote use in the Indian Territory, and its reemergence later would be at least partially responsible for the demise of Colony. During the summer of 1907, Henry accepted her invitation and came to Colony. In his memoirs he said, "I found myself in the midst of many of these Christian Indians. Since then I have never felt alone."[9]

It was also in Oklahoma that he met Walter Roe. Henry described him as "fearless, clear-headed, profoundly spiritual, (and) imprest me as a man whose soul was in line with the great movements of God. He labored against tremendous physical odds, yet he led an overflowing life of service for the Indian race."[10]

Two of the Christian Indians he met were Nahwats and Periconic—both of whom were Comanche. Mary Roe introduced Henry to them shortly after his arrival at Fort Sill. Both had spoken at a Lake Mohonk Conference in 1903. At that assembly Periconic said, "I begin to see the best thing I could do for my children is to give them schooling and let them learn all they can," and after imploring the audience to "give all you can for our young people, to give them schooling." Nahwarts concluded by saying that "I feel in my heart that you will do all can for the Indians. That is why I have come a long way, to ask you to do all you can for my people."[11] Both became influential leaders in the church.

Both had experience with mescal and peyote. Periconic told Henry. "I walked that road from the beginning almost to the end, and although many colds have gone by since I cut it off, my body is marked by Mescal." Nahwats said, "I was a priest of Mescal for thirty years. I followed that worship, and there is nothing in it. I saw visions, but they were dreams that fly away and leave the heart empty and small. Young man, go back to lead your tribe along the road that fills their hearts with joy."[12] Henry made the decision to go back to Winnebago for the rest of the summer to try to do just that.

Later that summer, while she was on a speaking tour, Mary Roe stopped by Winnebago to see Cloud. Together they went to the grave of William Findley—whose midnight visit while he was in school resulted in Henry's conversion to Christianity. Henry continued to lament about the moral decay that had plagued the Winnebago for the past quarter of a century. He specifically talked about how the value of land had increased to the point that the Indians found it more profitable to lease the land and live on the revenue than to farm the land to make it productive. According to him, theirs was now a culture of immorality and drunkenness. Before they left the gravesite, Henry and Mary read and reflected on the inscription that was on the grave maker: "My word shall not return unto me void,"[13] and although the exact path was not yet clear, the road that Henry Cloud was going to follow throughout the remainder of his life had been determined. His companions for a significant portion of that journey also had been determined. He began a relationship with Walter and Mary Roe that was personally and professionally life altering for him. Their relationship was so close that they informally adopted him, and he began using their name as part of his own. He changed his name to Henry Roe Cloud.

In some ways the Henry Cloud who returned to Yale for his sophomore year was a changed person. However, in many ways he and things in general, were the same. His schedule was still hectic and was becoming even more so. In addition to his course work, Bible studies, and fraternity life he was in great demand as a speaker. Largely depending on Walter Roe's network of friends in the east, Henry was frequently asked to travel to deliver speeches. He was still concerned about finances. To pay for his education at Yale Henry relied on lease money from land he had inherited on the Winnebago reservation. He also took on many different kinds of jobs. He collected tickets at ballgames and he waited tables. He increasingly was receiving money from the Roes. He also started selling Indian artifacts he and friends had collected in New England, but even more so, things that he acquired from friends and relatives on the reservation. Clark Wissler, an anthropologist who was in the Department of Ethnology at The American Museum of Natural History in New York tried to hire Henry to collect Winnebago artifacts for the museum, but Henry quickly realized that he could make more money selling the relics to individuals than by collecting them for a museum.

Cloud's grades continued to be above average, but not as good as he would have liked. He wrote Walter Roe about his continuing disappointment about not making Phi Beta Kappa. During his senior year he sent Mary Roe a description of a typical day for him at school. He rose, got dressed, and had breakfast before 8:00 am. At 8:10 he attended chapel. From 8:30 until 10:30 he studied law and philosophy. Between 10:30 and 11:30 he attended recitation in law. His philosophy of religion lecture class was from 11:30 until 12:30. At 12:30 he ate dinner. And after that attended what he described as a secret pray group until 1:30 pm. The next few hours were spent in philosophy of religion recitation. At 4:00 he bought tickets for a play that was to be held that Saturday, and then went to the gym to play a little handball. Another secret prayer group preceded supper at 6:00, and then he went to another prayer group after eating. At 7:30 he went to a classmate's room and read and studies for the next four hours before finally going to his room to go to bed. In another letter he described an Elihu meeting that concluded around 11:30, and he had not yet had time to prepare for the next day's classes.[14]

Another thing that interfered with his regular routine was his development of a preoccupation that was essentially becoming an obsession. His regular, and at one point daily, letters to Mary Roe revealed that he was increasingly frustrated with being away at school while so much needed to be done with the Roes and other missionaries among the Indians. On more than one occasion, even in the second semester of his senior he said that he should just "quit school and go to work when you need me so much."[15] Henry's life and future was becoming more intimately intertwined with the work and his relationship with the Roes. He was orphaned at age thirteen; they had lost an infant son who would have been just about Henry's age. Both became surrogates. Henry was becoming reliant on the educational and career advice of

Walter Roe. He was becoming more and more reliant on the connections Roe had in New York and New England. His relationship with Mary Roe was becoming closer. She was his confidant—a source of inspiration, support, and encouragement.

The next summer, 1908, Rev. Wright, the Roes, and Henry continued the work among the Winnebago. They were thought to be a very tough audience. The Roes said that they had seen more drunkenness in Winnebago that in their twelve years in the Southwest. Gambling was common among women as well as the men. Marriage was regarded as a mere temporary arrangement of convenience that could be set aside at the will of either. Throughout the month of July and into early August, they visited camps and homes in the area. Mary Roe called it "our little army of occupation." A central feature of their missionary work had become the camp meeting, and they began planning for it in August. After a great deal of debate and discussion, Walter Roe announced that the camp meeting was to be held on Flag Pole Hill—a place set aside for traditional Indian dances and worship. Cloud's advice and input were fundamental to that decision. They decided that it was very important that they show no fear of, or deference to, the traditional Medicine Lodge religion and its epicenter. Walter proclaimed that it was essential that they "strike at evil in its stronghold." To locate the camp meeting anywhere else would give de facto recognition to the sacred ground.

On Thursday, August 20, they pitched the tent and the camp meeting began. The first people who came were the Mescal men. They entered the tent and reverently sat down in the front rows. Most others, who came out a sense of curiosity more than real interest, stood around outside. One skeptic had told the missionaries that "you may talk for a thousand years but you will never gain one man from Medicine Lodge."[16] With that prediction in his mind, Henry called on his old skills as a coronet player and blew a bugle calling the assembly to order. The audience grew as they started singing hymns. As Rev. Wright stepped forward to begin, Hensley, the leader of the Mescal cult rose to speak. He said, "My friends, and you old men, hear me. It is the will of God that these people come to us." He went on to say that they were witnessing a change of power in their culture—they were losing it and the white men were gaining it. He then announced to Wright that he was prepared to join the church and to bring his 600 followers with him. When Walter Roe asked about mescal, Hensley said, "Mescal must come too."[17]

This presented a significant dilemma for the missionaries. They were strongly opposed to the use of mescal and peyote but were nevertheless aware that the cult did encourage the use of scripture and had undermined the Medicine Lodge and its monopoly of spirituality. Walter Roe was given to the use of analogies and examples. He responded, "If a man enters the army of the

White Father, he must choose which band he will enter. He may be a soldier who fights on foot, or he may belong to the soldiers who fight on horseback, or he may be one of the men who fights with great guns, but he cannot belong to any two of these at the same time. He must choose. . . when you joined Mescal you had to throw away your Medicine Lodge gods, and when you join us, you must throw away Mescal and worship God alone."[18]

Hensley's warning about the shifting alignment of power and Roe's clever use of the symbol of the United States army, coupled with the native understanding and admiration of the warrior culture seemed to resonant with the audience. That Sunday night a new church was established with 20 members.

Progress was being made in Winnebago and in the rest of the Indian Territory, but the challenges and problems were still there. The blending of Mescal and peyote with religion still existed among many. Alcohol had been an issue and would continue to be one for many years. The leasing of reservation land and the effect that it was having on native culture, initiative, and morality did not disappear. Indian education was still abysmal. Poor health and hygiene plagued the native peoples. It was clear that there was still much to do.

In May of 1909 Henry wrote an article for *The Yale Courant* about missions to the American Indians. In that article there is foreshadowing of just about everything that consumed Henry for the rest of his life.

> I speak in behalf of a vanishing race. I bear to you the gospel of Man's larger duty to Man. Strife has marked the development of the human family. It is a story of clash— of conflict—instead of brotherhood. Civilization, sure of its divine right, has extended the hand of fellowship to those outside its pale, only to let fall the mailed fist of the oppressor. In the name of enlightened progress I say the strong peoples of the earth must bear the burdens of the weak. What is to be the future of the American Indian? Is he to continue one of the petty pawns in the group of politics— more insignificant year by year—soothed on one hand by the sop of mawkish sentiment, later to be scourged for his transgressions to the utmost letter of the law? Can official wisdom find no solution of this grim problem? Is the last wigwam to pass from the prairies of the West before the curtain shall be rung down by this dark drama of blunder, injustice and greed?
>
> It does not become me here to indulge in bitterness over the methods by which the aborigines of this country were deprived of their domain. They but suffered the doom of the conquered. It is to their lasting glory that defeat did not break their spirit, and the ancient courage still survives, as defiant as when the colonial forests rang with their war cries. No—if I invoke history, it is not to lament the past, but to show the weakness, the Pecksniffian pretense of present policies toward the Indian.
>
> This background of history is not all shadow. The darkness is shot through and through with light. Good faith to last as long as the sun shone and rivers

flowed! This was the pledge the red man gave and to Penn alone was it sacred. A few others saw in this savage something besides a traditional foe. Under his gaudy war paint they beheld a human soul. The fierce spirit that refused to quail before the musket bullet yielded to the pleading of the missionary. Jesuit and Protestant alike found their way to the heart that had been filled with distrust of the invader. Under the guidance of the gentle Moravians the warrior laid down his tomahawk for the plow. The gods of storm and thunder gave way to the message of Christ. Around the council fire the chief passed the peace pipe even to his enemies. The Indian question was being solved. "I am my brother's keeper!" In that sublime phrase the early missionaries found a promise and a command. Into wild places, among savage beasts and still more savage men it led them to bear the tidings of Galilee. In the dim aisles of the forest, upon the bark of giant trees, Father Henning blazed the crucifix. Sustained by his unfaltering faith Brebauf died at the torture stake with a smile of hope upon his lips. Breathing a prayer of forgiveness the dauntless Lallemand gave his body to the flames. Shaking the raindrops from the ears of corn Marquette baptized the condemned Huron prisoners and they went to their death with a courage that made their captors marvel. Shall the dwindling numbers of the Indian make us forget John Eliot, the translator of the Bible? Are we to leave unfinished the work of the Mayhews of Martha's Vineyard, who father to son, for one hundred and sixty years, bore the torch of the Gospel? Is Yale to give us no more such champions as David Brainerd, or Jonathan Edwards, who stood at Stockbridge as the protector of the red man in the great French and English struggle for control?

These are the questions that cry out of the pages of history. And why? Because the Indian agent now stands in the place once held by the missionary—because the inspired message of the Bible has been supplanted by red tape! Between these two methods there is a gulf that cannot be measured. They cannot be operated in harmony. If you would reach the heart of the Indian, you must come to him with authority. To the agent belongs the power, while the missionary is forced to act by sufferance, dependent upon the whim and will of the official underling. It matters not that the agent is honest. That may alleviate, but it can never cure the evils of a faulty system. The Indian is a child in the human family. Appeal to his emotions— to the moral sense which is the common heritage of men, and in time he will grow to understand and respect the law. Give him spiritual leadership, instead of blankets and beef. The agency system as it now stands has been weighed in the balance and found wanting. It robs its charges of self-reliance; it makes paupers of those it is intended to aid.

The government has changed the conditions surrounding the Indian, but it has not changed his character. He has come in contact with a nation that represents thousands of years of progress, but even that has not saved him. The attempt to force upon him unconditionally the yoke of the white man's authority has fastened upon him the curse of the white man's vices. And the finished product of the government's care only too often is the shiftless drunkard of the reservation, or the blanket Indian in his teepee, a savage at heart. Under the brow of a hill in my own home, I can see a long, low wigwam. Here in their feathers and paint are gathered a thousand Indians, who have gone back to the gloom of paganism. I hear the dull thunder of the pigskin drum—the hiss and rattle of the beads in the shaken gourds. With weird chant, swaying to the wild rhythm of that strange music, the long line takes up its barbaric march. Faster and faster comes the beat of the drum, quickening the steps of the marchers, and in one mad whirl they encircle the hall until exhaustion ends the frenzy. Has twentieth century civilization nothing better than this for the red man? Shall the medicine lodge and the ghost dance regain their hold upon the hearts in which the Mission Fathers implanted the love of the living God?

On that same hill overlooking the barbaric orgies lies a lonely grave. The marble slab bears the words "William T. Findley, missionary to the Indians for sixteen years." Aye, Sixteen years so barren that he sobbed in anguish over His fruitless toil! He died, his great heart broken because those to whom he brought his message paid no heed to his words. They had ears only for the agent, clothed with temporal power.

Yet that noble life will not have been given in vain if it brings an awakening to the needs of the people he came to save. Send us—not soldiers nor agents—but men such as this. Give us Christian missions. Restore them to their dignity, so that those who bear the tidings of light may minister with freedom to those that sit in the darkness. In this way only will you lay the foundation for civic honor, respect for law and order, and purity in the home. Rebuilt those early Christian communities. Kindle anew those old fires of devotion. So shall the Indian gain the power to resist the vises that surround him. So shall this son of the older America remain to do honor to the land of his fathers.[19]

Henry's talent as a writer was becoming evident. In his article he included references to people who were missionaries to the Indians during the seventeenth and eighteenth century in New England and in Canada—including two, Brebauf and Lallemand—who were beaten to death while tied to stakes. He also mentioned the Mayhews of Martha's Vineyard, Thomas, Sr. and Thomas, Jr. Through their efforts the Vineyard Indians and many Nantucket Indians became professed Christians. In the 1630's, John Eliot He developed an interest in the Indian language and customs in the New England area, and he began to preach to the Indians around 1646. At first he preached in English but within a year he was preaching in their own tongue, Algonquian. Eliot published a catechism for them in 1654, and by 1658 he had translated the Bible into Algonquian becoming the first Bible to be printed in North America.

There was something more important than the readability of Henry's article, its historically appealing content, or its missionary zeal. Henry Roe Cloud, a Winnebago Indian attending Yale, was becoming a voice people listened to about the plight of the American Indian. It was becoming clear that he was developing the reputation of a person who should and would figure prominently into efforts to solve some of those problems. It was also becoming evident that Cloud himself was close to accepting what he interpreted as a calling to become such a figure. What was not clear to Henry, however, was the path he should take in doing so.

NOTES

1. Elizabeth M.Page, *In Camp and Tepee,* (New York: Fleming H. Revell Company, 1915), 69.
2. LeRoy Koopman,*Taking the Jesus Road,* (Cambridge: William B. Eerdman Publishing Company, 2005), 75.
3. Koopman, *Taking the Jesus Road,* 81.
4. Page, *In Camp and Tepee,* 122.
5. Page, *In Camp and Tepee,* 123.
6. Henry Roe Cloud to Mary Roe, 16 January 1910, Roe Family Papers, Yale University Library, New Haven, Connecticut.
7. Page, *In Camp and Tepee,* 196.
8. Ibid.,195.
9. Henry Roe Cloud, "From Wigwam to Pulpit," *Missionary Review of the World*, (May 1915), 14.
10. Ibid., 14.
11. William J.Rose, "Remarks of Nehwarts," *Proceedings of the Twenty-second Annual Meeting,* (Lake Mohonk: The Lake Mohonk Conference, 1904), 56.
12. Page, *In Camp and Tepee,* 198.
13. Ibid.,200.
14. Henry Roe Cloud to Mary Roe, 13 January 1910, Roe Family Papers, Yale University Library, New Haven, Connecticut.
15. Ibid.
16. Page, *In Camp and Tepee,* 204.
17. Ibid., 207.
18. Ibid., 206-207.
19. Henry Roe Cloud, "Missions to the American Indians," *The Yale Courant,* May 1909, (New Haven, Connecticut): 520-523.

Chapter Nine

Choosing Roads

Oral tradition and published literature are replete with the idea of people having to choose which path or roads to take. Wo-Na-Xi-Lay-Hunka's grandmother told him the story of the Creek Indian who became a "preaching listener" and then had to decide which road to take in his last travel. Missionaries tried to convince Indians to take the "Jesus road." Less than five years after Cloud graduated from Yale, Robert Frost wrote "The Road Not Taken;" perhaps the most famous example of this analogy. During his last years at Yale, Henry Roe Cloud precariously balanced his time, his energy, and his emotions between often conflicting forces. His college life, and all that it entailed, demanded a great deal. His financial insecurity bothered him much of the time. His different ways of dealing with money problems—loans, speaking engagements, selling artifacts, and gifts from the Roes, weighed heavily on his emotions and often created problems with the best way to use his time. And as graduation loomed, Henry now had to decide what exactly to do after his years at Yale came to an end. Unlike most of his native contemporaries, Henry had choices. However, sometimes having those choices presented greater problems to Henry than having none at all. Henry Roe Cloud's decision-making, as was true of his life in general, was so inextricably tied to that of the Roes at this time that the best way to see how he made those decisions is to look at his correspondence to and from them. Walter seldom lacked advice, and Mary seldom lacked a compassionate ear. Walter Roe's letters to Henry were often dictated to, and written by, Mary. Occasionally Walter utilized a typewriter. Henry made several attempts at using the "Oliver machine" himself, but confessed that the outcome was often a "quire letter"[1] and that he often got commas where he needed periods.

Writing in December of 1909, Walter addressed both the issue of Henry's "financial tether" and the road he might take after graduation. Walter always encouraged Henry to participate in as many activities at Yale as he could handle, but began to question the value of Henry's membership in the Elihu Club. Perhaps the nature of being a secret society precluded his understanding exactly what it was, but he thought that it came at a pretty high cost in terms of money and time. He cautioned Henry that being an officer (secretary) in it might become a boa constrictor to Henry. Walter confessed that he feared debt like a rattlesnake and hoped that Henry's trust funds and the profits from selling Indian rugs and belts might provide some much needed relief. In that letter he also suggested that Henry had told Mary about problems he was having with his teeth. However, the bulk of the letter dealt with a review and analysis of the various prospects for Henry's future. Cloud had previously discussed with both Walter and Mary the possibility of working with the Y.M.C.A. or teaching at Hampton Institute, but had recently conveyed to Mary regarding these possibilities that the "fire is already out." A more intriguing possibility involved teaching at Robert College, an American secondary school, in Constantinople (Istanbul) Turkey. Walter confessed that this prospect was intriguing, but probably not practical for someone like Henry who was not going to be a writer, an editor, a minister, or a lawyer—professions that he thought were too general for a person of Henry's calling. He said that, "your fix is rather different from that of most college fellows, in that God has distinctly lined out to you, by His Providence of birth, training, and opportunity, a clearly defined sphere of action. Earlier than is true of most young men He has made you a specialist, with a significant field of activity before you. Your College and Seminary courses will give you sufficient general culture combined with your intercourse with cultivated people, to fit you for the work that lies before you, and all time spent upon lines of general cultivation from this time on it seems to me are but deflecting from the straight line towards your ultimate goal. . . you are already started upon a definite journey, which leads to the up-lifting of the Indian race, and more and more you must focus on that point. It further seemed to me that your people need you. This is a critical time when the tribe is hanging in the balance, and they have a right to look to you for your presence and help at this critical time."[2]

It is interesting to note that Walter Roe did not seem at all reluctant to try to reinforce the sense of responsibility that Henry was already feeling toward his people. It is interesting to note that, in his correspondence during this time period, Henry Cloud occasionally refers to himself by using his Indian name—Wo-Na-Xi-Lay-Hunka. In her 2004, work *Keepers of the Children: Native American Wisdom and Parenting*, Laura Rameriz says that "a spiritual name gives him (a Native American child) a sense of responsibility to himself and to others because he has a name that he must live up to and a purpose to unfold. . . A spiritual name gives him a sense of meaning and direction. Within his nature are the seeds of his awakening—his identity, means of belonging, and contribution to the whole."³ Henry had said that his native name meant War Chief. Clearly, Henry shared Walter and Mary Roe's opinion that he was destined to be a leader of importance for his people.

Both Walter and Mary wrote Henry letters on January 12, 1910. They wrote in response to a letter that Mary received from Henry that came that same day. She described Henry's tone in that letter as being very blue. Actually, Mary wrote both but wrote across one that it was "dictated by father." They generally dealt with the same issues but approached them very differently. The money problems had not been resolved. Walter encouraged Henry to follow-up on letters that he had been written requesting his portion of tribal funds. He also referenced Henry's concern with not being in Phi Beta Kappa by saying that "it would be nice to have if it should come your way, but do not strain unduly after it or grieve too deeply if you fail to bag it. A great many men who did not get a key have done something in the world at large." He talked about his and Mary's improving health and mentioned that he was now using a listening device, which he called a gramophone, which seemed to work although it was quite expensive. Mary, on the other hand, began her letter by saying that she was going to "get a lever under some of these things which burden you so much and lift them outright." She encouraged him not to give up about Phi Beta Kappa and to "do your best bravely and happily and leave the result with God." She concluded by saying, "I will love you laddie "to the never ending future. Nothing will rob you of my love. And we will share both our joys and sorrows, and both will draw us closer to one another. Mother loves you tonight with her whole heart and has thought in both this letter and in points suggested to Father, just how to ease your burden."⁴ The next night, Thursday January 13, 1910, Henry wrote Mary just after he returned from Elihu Club. He told her than within an hour and a half the Scroll and Key Men (A secret society along the lines of Skull and Bones) would start their regular Thursday night ritual of singing their song—Song of the Troubadours. He said, "O Mother, many a Thursday night I am stirred to the depths of my soul as I lay awake and hear that song coming the instant the chapel clock strikes 12:30. 'Singing from Palestine hither I come—lady love, lady love, welcome home.' Had I gone to Constantinople I would have been singing those very words to you on my way back across those Oriental lands." Mother, someday love may grip me for some girl but I love you just the same for all time. I'll sing that song to you in my heart this night."⁵ The generally accepted words to the song are:

> Gaily the troubadour touch his guitar,
> As he was hastening home from the war,
> Singing from Palestine, hither I come,
> Lady love, lady love, welcome me home.

Later that same day, and perhaps in a more loquacious mood, Henry wrote a 27 page missive to Mary. He compared himself to a "wayfarer trying to work his way through a thicket, laboriously lifting one leg over the underbrush, logs and whatnot. . . (with) his head down into the thicket with eyes closed and arms uplifted. If you can imagine the thicket as jammed into my brain and forming there a tangle of worries each long twig, some strong thread of worry, you can see something of the state. . . I was in all that time." He went on to talk about his being short of funds and that $40.00 had been stolen from him while he was in New York. Rather than share his misfortune with people around him, Henry decided to remain silent and try to pretend that everything was fine. This masquerade during the Christmas holiday season apparently plunged him into a period of depression and self-doubt. He told Mary that he was especially sorry that his frame of mind had kept him from writing her and that he had "failed to express my love for you." He said that his "little lies" had made him hate himself even more. To his credit he then said that he should not gone on that way and that (after many weeks and 17 pages of self-pity) it was time to look on the bright side of things. He had asked for and had received a no interest loan for two hundred dollars from Miss Sarah Dixon. He had received a fifty dollar check from Mary. He resolved to put that money in a savings bank in order to be able to send it back if the Roes needed it. He continued on with a detail account of how he was spending his time and concluded by saying "I'll never stop if I don't stop which is self-evident. So here I'm going to stop." He then continued on asking about a misplaced ring and several other matters. Clearly, Henry had a lot that he wanted to say to Mrs. Roe.[6]

The near-daily correspondence continued with a letter from Mary Roe written on January 14, 1910. She began by saying that she had just put his recent letters in order by date. She indicated that the order in which they had been received was not the same order in which they had been written contributing to some confusion and distress. The emotional outpourings of the letters did not always correspond to what had most recently been written by the other person. Mary even suggested that she had considered using the telegraph. She elaborated a little about Walter's continuing health problems expressing the hope that they might avert another serious attack. She said that she was "trying, oh so hard to forget myself and all my own cares and be happy and strong and cheerful for Father's sake, and yours Laddie, and my people here who suffer so when I give out even for a day. . . I feel your troubles, as I do Father's, in every nerve and tissue of my sensitive mind and body."[7] She wrote Henry another letter that was dated the same day. In that letter she encouraged Henry to not try to write her every day. She felt that it would be better to write on Sundays and perhaps once or twice in between

Sundays. She said that "if you get me used to daily letters, then when they stop for a fortnight of course I fear you are sick or in trouble some way. You know that I love the letters but I feel that you should not take too fast a pace." Walter had become sick again, and Mary said that "it is hard to bear. . . It keeps my heart so heavy to watch him suffer." During his sick periods, Mary said that she spent her days in "semi-darkness, "and that those days "mean(s) a long letter for you, because it comforts my heart to write you when I feel so alone." These letters plainly revealed Mary Roe's love for Henry and her dedication to the work of her husband.[8]

In his Sunday night, January 16, 1910, letter Henry told Mary Roe that he had had dinner that afternoon with Dr. Angier who was an assistant professor in the Psychology Department. There he ran into one of his old teachers at Santee Mission School—Edith M. Dabb. Miss Dabb was the Secretary for Indian Work with the Young Women's Christian Association. Henry told his mother that he thought that Miss Dabb could "help us a lot." He also said that since she was a young lady he could not talk freely with her on the topic of the girls with whom she works.[9] Like many of her contemporaries who worked with Native Americans, Miss Dabb had participated in various Lake Mohonk Conferences. In 1908, she reported to the conference about the work the Y.W.C.A. was doing, and in 1916 her statement that "women must be made to feel that it (Indian education) is a profession worthy of their taking up, worthy of their giving their lives to, and a profession which really is recognized by education people throughout the country as one worthy of being studied" was greeted with sustained applause.[10] She contributed to *The Handbook of the American Indian and His Art* in 1934 but took the position that native dances were a waste of time and that sentimentalists who continue to dwell on the beauties of the quaint and primitive world should remember that primitive beauty is frequently found in close company with primitive cruelty and primitive ugliness. She added that "Indian dancing was a primary cause of the downfall of young girls."[11] In 1944 Ella Deloria acknowledged Miss. Dabb in *Speaking of Indians* for her "breadth of knowledge and wealth of experience."[12] In 1910 Henry certainly thought that Edith was a "fine woman" and encouraged the Roes to welcome her warmly to Colony when she visited in February. Henry takes the occasion of this letter to mention a couple of other interesting things. First he told Mary that he had started wearing his moccasins, presumably a gift, for the first time, and he told her that it was prom week in New Haven. He said that he found all of the pretty girls to be bewitching, but that he was going to the prom stag using a ticket one of the other students had given him. He concluded the letter by saying that he had to stop in order to go work on getting an acting club started, and it seems like he was perhaps auditioning for the club as well. This letter gives the distinct impression that Henry was trying very hard to be positive and it was superficially upbeat being written only three days after a morose letter in which he confessed that he felt "unnatural."[13]

On January 18, 1910, Mary wrote Henry saying that "Mother understands you. Dear you know me well enough to know that I have the same things to fight—moods, blues, the bad heart, which with Indians, as you well know, is caused not always by sin, but more often by grief, disappointment, jealousy, and other causes. Henry, this indulgence is the bad heart both you and I for Christ's sake, because it is so un-Christlike, selfish, inconsiderate to those nearest to us, must root-out, root and branch, if it grows in us clear down to our hearts." She acknowledged that while he was trying to appear outwardly happy, those whose vision had grown sharper because of "anxious love" would know that something was wrong. As was the case in most of her letters she again told him not to worry about his finances and assured him that they would help. She cautioned him that his senior year would be the most expensive one. She told him that "no boy ever had a father more broadly and sweetly reasonable than yours." As always she assured him that her love was strong and never-ending. Her letter also addressed Henry's impending graduation from college. She had received his class ring and was going to send it to him along with a couple of ideas about what to have engraved on it. She suggested his initials and the Chi Rho, one of the earliest christograms used by Christians. She also said that she felt that Henry was learning something important about life by her constant professions of love and concern. She said, "In trying to show you how to deal with me in tenderness and consideration, I feel, my son, that you are learning a lesson upon which you own life happiness may some day hang. Mother('s) love is so constant, so steadfast. As life goes on and we feel how love can come and go, be born and die, those loves which last will rest us where our souls are dreary."[14] She might have been preparing Henry for the inevitable broken heart most young men experience; she might have preparing him for the difficulties he might experience as a person who was essentially caught between cultures; or perhaps this was Mary Roe's way of telling Henry that Walter's health was still failing and that more difficult times were ahead.

From mid-January until early May, both Henry and Mary indicated that a "mist" fell between them. Both of the Roes had prolonged periods of illness, and no doubt the intensity of the work they were doing had something to do with that. Their efforts were expanding among the Comanche and the Apache. They were trying to find missionaries to lead these endeavors. There were financial and internal organizational problems within the mission board. They spoke about a five or six thousand dollar deficit. Walter was becoming increasingly involved with the Jicarilla Apache as well as with the plight of the imprisoned, then exiled, now homeless Chiricahua Apache. Walter had been involved in their plight for several years. Elizabeth Page said that Dr. Roe was given the task of examining their aging leader, Geronimo, after he formally converted to Christianity in 1903. This conversion was not believed, welcomed, or even accepted by many who had seen acts of atrocity that he had been responsible for earlier, but Roe said, after questioning him deeply and carefully, that "no consistory in our church could refuse to admit a man to membership after such a confession."[15]

Likewise Henry was occupied with his regular college routines and activities. His frequent speaking engagements and on-going efforts to raise money for both the Roe's work and his own needs took more and more of his time. Walter Roe expressed his (and Mother's) concern about the speeches and suggested that Henry become more focused on his school work. In early May, the mist began to lift, and the frequency and depth of the letters increased.

Both Walter and Mary Roe wrote letters to Henry on May 4, 1910. He had written them about a visit he had made to the Hill School in Pottstown, Pennsylvania. The differences in these letters seem to reflect the different dispositions of the two writers in addition to the different type of relationship Henry had with each. After briefly mentioning that the four years the Roes had spent at the school in Pottstown were "useful and in the main happy years in our lives," Walter added briefly that Mary's nearly fatal illness and the death of their son there cast a shadow over "their brightness." He then talked about the spiritual strength of John Meigs, the school's principal and his wife Marion Butler Meigs. At that point Walter predictably moved on to the issue of what Henry might or should do after his graduation from Yale.[16] Mary, on the other hand, used over half of her letter to reflect on the events at Hill School. She talked in considerably more detail about her illness and their son's death, and what Marion Meigs (Mrs. John) had done during that time. While Mary was ill, Marion breast fed the infant Roe child along with her own child. He then told Henry about the questionable character of Marion's mother and the uninspiring model her father, Cyrus, was. Mary attributed Marion's greatness to her beloved Nurse Eunice. Mary said that she and Marion were made out of "different clay," and that she did not feel worthy to touch her shoes. Strangely, the normally forthright Mary had never been able to talk about it to Marion. Then just as quickly as Walter shifted to the matters than concerned him most—spiritual diligence, responsibility, and finances—Mary shifted to those things that mattered most to her—Henry and their relationship.[17]

Henry Roe Cloud had said that he wanted to be a "leader among my people." In this letter, Walter Roe's question to him was, "Well, what kind of leader?" It is very likely that Henry was able to anticipate what would come next. After discussing the various types of leadership need among the Indians and the different skill sets and knowledge that were needed for each, Walter reasoned that religious leadership was the best answer and that "it would seem to me that what you need is to be saturated with religious knowledge, spiritual zeal, practical power to use the Bible, and a strong ground-work of theological training, especially for your own benefit, and your association with white men, and yet, who knows... you might have to organize an Indian theological seminary to train native workers to go out among their tribes?" Then he added that Henry would need to look into his heart, but that he and Mother (Mary) thought that he should spend two years at Oberlin Theological Seminary and the study in Scotland for the third year of study—Scotland being the birthplace of Presbyterianism. Several times in the letter Walter preface his opinion and suggestions with the phrase, "mother and I' showing Henry that they are in agreement and suggesting that she is present at its writing—which, in fact, she was. In her next letter Mary indicates that the letter was dictated by "father." The letter was typed. "Walter" concludes the letter with "mother sends her greetings."[18]

Mary's mention in her letter about the unsavory background of Marion's mother and her undistinguished father was not so much a commentary about them as it was praise for her. It was also an effective way to transition to a discussion about heredity and "blood" for Henry's sake. She said, "I have often told you my son how your coming into your close and sacred relation to me had already done much to heal an open wound in the loss of my baby boy. I believe I would rather have you with just the blood that does run in your veins, It spells opportunity to you. It points out your battleground, but also your chance of leading on to a victory. It pulls down sometimes... but it ought to put a terrific leverage of thought to move you to almost superhuman effort. Your blood gives you your mission." She went on to say that she loved Henry, not in spite of his inheritance, but more because of it. "You do not yet fully understand me, dear Henry, and I do not always understand you, but love and patience, and tender gentleness, forgiveness that comes instantly before being asked, prayer and communion, duties draught out together, burdens carried side by side—these in the passing years will soon enter into the bed-rock of our characters and we shall see clearly, 'know even as also we are known'." Mary consistently and intentionally reinforced the idea that Henry was going to be a leader of his "people." In this same letter she "reverently" compared the native blood coursing through Henry's veins to the blood or the human inheritance of sin that flowed to Jesus from his mother. She added to Henry that his (Jesus) example could be an impenetrable shield. She added that she was in another nervous condition, but that she would try to regain her strength for a trip back east for his graduation.[19]

Mary's next letter to Henry was written the next day. She had obviously written her letter of the previous day before Walter dictated his. In this May 5 letter she said that yesterday Walter had been fighting off a serious headache, and that she had devoted her time to him yesterday—the twelve page letter to Henry notwithstanding. She describe how Walter had paced back and forth in his room as he talked about Henry's future and that of his "race," She praised Walter for his world view and cautioned Henry to beware the advice of people who saw things as more important than they really were because they were so close to them. She urged Henry to save that letter and refer to it for consul. The rest of her letter was unusually business-like and dealt with organization matters associated with the Women's Board of Missions and their Indian work.[20]

Henry's May 5th letter was far from business-like. It began: "I wonder what you are doing now. I love you dearly." The intensity of this letter does not diminish any from that point. He wrote, "As the days fleet past one by one, I get impatient for the time when we shall be together. You know it will be only for three weeks at the longest and that time is so short. I stay in Winnebago and you go home to the southern Indians. We are separated again in a short time. Then the next year I must be away again perhaps in Scotland—at any rate away off somewhere. I feel we must get together. Try as we will a mysterious gap comes in the longer we are separated. I do not mean that this gap separates us. No, but we do not have the consciousness of growth together. It is so in the case of every two people who come together suddenly, loved, and then as quickly separated again. The love is the same but the attitude is gradually changing intellectually. We will find perhaps that we have not changed as much as we think. But the glorious times we will have together! Alone together! Being with sweet, godly people as the Meigs. Could anything be better? As you often say, 'Two to the world for the world's work sake'."He signed the letter, "With sweet love, Mother. Your boy, Wo-Na-Xi-Lay-Hunka."[21]

Henry's response to the Roe's letters of May 4th was both lyrical and revealing. He started the letter on Sunday before church, worked on it after church, and finished it Monday night. It had been raining in New Haven. He wrote, "I saw women gathering their skirts up and also saw birds on the walls all cramped into themselves trying their best to shed the big drops that persist in trying to get under their feathers. . . Everything seemed to protest against this unwelcome intrusion of the rain. The trolley as they roared by spit blue flames of fire from the wires overhead and from the wheels underneath. . . Great big drops of water would slowly gather, drop and another would follow along the noses of the statues on the campus." He talked about looking forward to taking her to Elihu when she came to visit. He told Mary that her letter was a great one and that it had encouraged him, comforted him, made him feel more hopeful, and inspired him. He concluded by acknowledging Walter's "strong, splendid" letter and that he thought he was right in his advice. He went to bed after completing the letter in order to get plenty of rest for the oratorical contest the next day.[22] On May 10th, the next day, Henry sent a telegram to the Roes:

New Haven Conn May10th1910
Dr. & Mrs Walter C Roe.
Colony, Okla.
Lost gold prize close second mastery over self great victory.
                                    Henry[23]

In Mary's May 11th letter, she called Henry's note of May 5th, the "first natural spontaneous letter" that she had received from him in a long time. She had written and then destroyed three different letters the previous Sunday because she was too sick to safely be sure what she was writing. She wrote again about the "baffling, bewildering mist" that had existed between them, but she added that now she felt that they would brush it away as soon as they were together. In fact, she indicated that until she received this last letter she was becoming less certain about coming to visit for his graduation. She felt the need for "these days with you in sweet natural companionship." She revealed that she had been asked to come to New York by the Executive Secretary of the National Board of the Y.M.C.A., but that Father had told her that she could not be spared at Colony. However, she did see the opportunity to come to Boston and asked Henry to go with her. She passed on some advice from Walter who suggested that Henry use Western Union instead of the Postal Telegraphy Company of Texas. They had received his telegram, and it read "Mrs. Loss. Gold prize. Close second mastery overfell great victory."

She said that she had been sick for nearly ten days with a terrible headache like the one she had in Winnebago. Walter had taken care of her and had apparently overdone it himself. He "came down on Mon. and spent Tues. and Wed. in bed." She told Henry that his help and good cheer was essential for her well-being. She was planning on bringing several books on her trip for Henry to read to her. Like before the mist, she concluded with professions of love. "Mother's love is sure and steadfast and has never flickered all the winter. . . Henry it is not what you do not tell, but what you cannot tell which means danger always in the close relations of life. . . I love you, my son, with a love which through the passing weeks of my year of usual distress of many kinds, is becoming more worthy. It must have its hours of suffering before it comes of any worth. It is so with true love."[24]

Two days later, Mary wrote another long letter to Henry. She talked about the rainy Sunday he described so lyrically. They were experiencing severe weather in Colony. A hot, dry winter from the south alternated with a cold freezing one from the north leaving crops dead in their wake. The corrected telegram had confirmed what the Roes surmised about Henry's placing second in the oratorical contest. Mary said that Father thought that it was too late for a congratulatory letter, but she wanted Henry to know that she was very proud of him. She said that in return for her congratulations, she wanted Henry's commensurations. She revealed a stubborn streak as she told him about her on-going wrangling with the express company over a dress that she had made but which was destroyed in delivery. She said that she would push them for over a year if necessary and that she had charged them thirty dollars for their carelessness.[25]

Mary and Henry kept up this every other day letter exchange until it was time for her to come to New Haven for his graduation. Often the letters did little more than reassure each other of their love. Once Mary told Henry that she needed to develop an entirely new vocabulary in dealing with him—common words were insufficient. She said that she had a new name for him—it was Navin. She added that it was equally applicable if he wanted to call her that. Most sources indicate that the name Navin originally meant new or novel. She then asked Henry more pointedly for the Indian word for "Torchbearer," because "I feel a torch has been put into your hands which no other Indian hand clasps today"[26]—not even Charles Eastman.

He wrote her about sermons and speeches he had heard and thoughts he had as he was thinking about them later. He described himself as a "young man who up to this time has found the struggle almost not worthwhile. One is tempted to say 'What's the use?'" however, he then talked about the great scientists and the great poets, who believe in immortality and who "were not satisfied with this world any more than a flower would (be) in a flower pot." He quickly changed to the topics of plays he had seen and events that were coming up on campus. There were to be parades, tug of war, three legged races, and all sorts of costumes. He was planning on wearing his Indian "paraphernalia," including a Sioux war bonnet. Thursday, May 19, was going to be tap day under the elm tree. That was the day men were tapped for the secret societies Skull and Bones, Scroll and Key, Wolf's Head, and Elihu. Then strangely he says, "Mother unless you feel that God does not want you to come, do not come, and be certain of it too." Perhaps he did not say what he was trying to say, but he added "God's will be done in any case. It seems to me that I could not be very easily reconciled to anything less than God's will. . . I know God will let you come. I'm praying that he may. We will have wonderful times together. . . So goodnight dear. You are more to me than you realize. This writer's work has not been in vain."[27] His normally articulate prose seems to have failed him in the last portion of this May 16th letter. The anticipation of the events surrounding graduation and the visit from Mary seems to have affected him deeply.

In one letter Henry talked about the "doings" of college life and remarked that he had gotten into the festivities wholeheartedly. Dressed in his war bonnet he had entertained at a baseball game going so far as to "scalp" the umpire whenever he made a bad call. He had recovered from his uncertainties of the previous day and wrote, "It makes me very happy that you have decided to come. I do not think that it will be a mistake. You need rest and change and your coming will take away the string of my graduating from Yale,-nothing but an orphan, without mother and father to appreciate in this world. Sometimes the pessimistic feeling comes to me,—if you have no one to share, in love, the good things of joy, of achievement, of love, of suffering, of what good is it? . . . I will send this off so you will get it by Saturday. This letter has been perfumed with love inside and out for you, dear."[28]

The frequency of the use of the word love in correspondence between Henry and Mary cannot be understated or overlooked. There was no doubt a strong emotional attachment that went beyond what might be thought of as normal in an adoptive—although informally so—mother and son relationship. Owing to the frequent separations, her marital status, her frequent health and emotional issues, it is highly doubtful that the relation had been consummated through anything other than letters and professions of love. Likewise, it is conceivable that her coming to his graduation without Walter might present an opportunity for the relationship to become something other than what it had been. She wrote, "So it will not be long now before I see you. We have not lived our deepest lives together for many weeks, altho(sic) we have wanted to, have tried to, and have clung to one another all the same. It will not be hard to make clear much that now baffles us, so do not worry, but make the most and best. . ."[29]

Mary's constant emphasis on the position of responsibility and leadership that she feels Henry is destined to have with "his people" is evident through her letters as well. She advised him to take full advantage of his last days of "your boy life. The stern pressure of responsibility comes soon enough, and it was your right to have it."[30]

Unfortunately, Henry did not get a chance to participate in the commencement ceremony with the rest of his class. His anticipated bucolic days of wandering down New England roads, trekking through dim forests, and sitting beside rivers with Mary did not happened. He spent the next few weeks recovering from an emergency appendectomy. He was stricken with appendicitis as he was finishing his last exam. In letters to Walter Roe, Elizabeth Page, and others he refused to feel sorry for himself and instead interpreted the illness as a message from God. He said, "please do not feel sorry in your good times for me. I have nothing to complain of. Usually one misses only what they value when they are taken away. All that I value, I have, so I can bear the rest."[31] He declared that by the end of July he was going west—for good. In many ways, Henry seemed relieved and perhaps reflected on the potential perniciousness of his relationship with Mary.

During his convalescence at Dr. Cheney's Sanatorium in New Haven, Mary Roe visited him daily. On June 29, just after Mary left the hospital for dinner at 8:00 p.m. and before he returned later, Henry took the occasion to write a letter to Walter. In that letter he addressed clinically what he thought might be troubling Mary. He said it this way, "As I diagnose her case, I see it this way." First, she was having unnamed physical ailments that might be minor at the present, but which might require surgery sometime in the future. He described her as being naturally high strung or nervous not unlike a thoroughbred horse, and like the horse that characteristic is what have her strength. He then said that "I find now that he trouble is her relations with people in general. In this case, Father it is her relations with me that has caused all the trouble. I can see that her physical trouble is the resultant of the warped and distorted relations which I have brought about myself this year. Mother would never get sick if her loved ones loved her as faithfully and as strongly as she has a right to expect. We have righted everything, Father, and she is now happy as a singing lark on the wing." Then he told Walter about an encounter with a "temptress." The night before he was to lead the university's Y.M.C.A. meeting, he met a girl who invited him to Mount Carmel which was located a few miles out of New Haven. Their plan was to meet at 3:00 on Sunday. The next day, Mac Vilas, the General Secretary of the Y.M.C.A. asked Henry to lead a meeting organized by Robert Speer who was active in both the Y.M.C.A. and the Student Volunteer Movement or SVM. Henry said that he told Vilas that he was "not a big enough man" to handle the responsibility while knowing that the real reason was his plan to meet the girl. Finally, he agreed to do it but met the girl as well. Although he was not proud of it, the only thing that prevented him from succumbing to the girl after "putting myself in temptation's way" was the responsibility of the meeting. According to Henry, the net result of the whole experience was that he hated himself, and that feeling that way he could not write to "Mother" the way that he should. The "soul had gone out" of his letters. He also revealed in that letter than Mary had become jealous of her sister, Elizabeth Page, and suspected her of trying to replace her in Henry's heart.[32] Henry's confession about his temptation seemed to resolve that issue, and family unity was restored. The mist had risen and apparently the air had been cleared. Henry Roe Cloud was anxious to get back to Winnebago and then begin the next phase of his life.

NOTES

1. Henry Roe Cloud to Mary Roe, 9 April 1911, Roe Family Papers, Yale University Library, New Haven, Connecticut.

2. Walter Roe to Henry Roe Cloud, 7 December 1909, Roe Family Papers, Yale University Library, New Haven, Connecticut.

3. Laura M.Ramierz, *Keepers of the Children: Native American Wisdom and Parenting,* (Reno: Walk in Peace Productions, 2004.), 72.

4. Walter Roe and Mary Roe to Henry Roe Cloud, 12 January 1910, Roe Family Papers, Yale University Library, New Haven, Connecticut.

5. Henry Roe Cloud to Mary Roe, 13 January 1910, Roe Family Papers, Yale University Library, New Haven, Connecticut.

6. Henry Roe Cloud to Mary Roe, 13 January 1910, Roe Family Papers, Yale University Library, New Haven, Connecticut.

7. Mary Roe to Henry Roe Cloud, 14 January 1910, Roe Family Papers, Yale University Library, New Haven, Connecticut.

8. Mary Roe to Henry Roe Cloud, 14 January 1910, Roe Family Papers, Yale University Library, New Haven, Connecticut.

9. Henry Roe Cloud to Mary Roe, 16 January 1910, Roe Family Papers, Yale University Library, New Haven, Connecticut.

10. "Remarks," *Report of the Thirty-fourth Annual Lake Mohonk Conference* (The Lake Mohonk Conference, 1916), 54.

11. Tisa Wegner, *We Have a Religion: The 1920s Pueblo Indian Dance Controversy and American Religious Freedom,* (Chapel Hill: The University of North Carolina Press, 2009), 175.

12. Ella Deloria, *Speaking of Indians,* (Lincoln: University of Nebraska Press, 1998), Acknowledgment.

13. Henry Roe Cloud to Mary Roe, 13 January 1910, Roe Family Papers, Yale University Library, New Haven, Connecticut.

14. Mary Roe to Henry Roe Cloud, 14 January 1910, Roe Family Papers, Yale University Library, New Haven, Connecticut.

15. LeRoy Koopman,*Taking the Jesus Road* (Cambridge: William B. Eerdman Publishing Company, 2005), 117.

16. Walter Roe to Henry Roe Cloud, 4 May 1910, Roe Family Papers, Yale University Library, New Haven, Connecticut.

17. Mary Roe to Henry Roe Cloud, 14 January 1910, Roe Family Papers, Yale University Library, New Haven, Connecticut.

18. Walter Roe to Henry Roe Cloud, 4 May 1910, Roe Family Papers, Yale University Library, New Haven, Connecticut.

19. Mary Roe to Henry Roe Cloud, 14 January 1910, Roe Family Papers, Yale University Library, New Haven, Connecticut.

20. Mary Roe to Henry Roe Cloud, 5 May 1910, Roe Family Papers, Yale University Library, New Haven, Connecticut.

21. Henry Roe Cloud to Mary Roe, 5 May 1910, Roe Family Papers, Yale University Library, New Haven, Connecticut.

22. Henry Roe Cloud to Mary Roe, 9 May 1910, Roe Family Papers, Yale University Library, New Haven, Connecticut.

23. Henry Roe Cloud telegram to Dr. and Mrs. Walter Roe, 10 May 1910, Roe Family Papers, Yale University Library, New Haven, Connecticut.

24. Mary Roe to Henry Roe Cloud, 11 May 1910, Roe Family Papers, Yale University Library, New Haven, Connecticut.

25. Mary Roe to Henry Roe Cloud, 13 May 1910, Roe Family Papers, Yale University Library, New Haven, Connecticut.

26. Mary Roe to Henry Roe Cloud, 15 May 1910, Roe Family Papers, Yale University Library, New Haven, Connecticut.

27. Henry Roe Cloud to Mary Roe, 16 May 1910, Roe Family Papers, Yale University Library, New Haven, Connecticut

28. Henry Roe Cloud to Mary Roe, 17 May 1910, Roe Family Papers, Yale University Library, New Haven, Connecticut.

29. Mary Roe to Henry Roe Cloud, 20 May 1910, Roe Family Papers, Yale University Library, New Haven, Connecticut.

30. Mary Roe to Henry Roe Cloud, 20 May 1910, Roe Family Papers, Yale University Library, New Haven, Connecticut.

31. Henry Roe Cloud to Elizabeth Page, 24 June 1910, Roe Family Papers, Yale University Library, New Haven, Connecticut.

32. Henry Roe Cloud to Walter Roe, 29 June 1910, Roe Family Papers, Yale University Library, New Haven, Connecticut

Chapter Ten

The World Outside the Classroom, 1902–1910

After he left Nebraska for Mount Hermon, the world of Henry Cloud expanded dramatically. His contacts with the "outside world" grew exponentially. He read more, he travelled more, he heard more, and he saw more than most American Indians of his time. He participated in organizations like the Cosmopolitan Club that were organized expressly for the purpose of promoting international and intercultural understanding. However, at the same time he was becoming more and more focused on the conditions of Indians in the United States. He thought about studying in Scotland or teaching in Turkey, but those things never materialized. His writing, personal correspondence and articles alike, dealt with the singular issue of the condition of the American Indian and the multitude of complications present in that condition. It would be presumptuous to suggest that he was unaware or even uninterested in other things that were happening, but no records exist to show that he invested much time or thought in them. There are many things that happened during the time period 1902–1910 that help place his preoccupations in historical perspective.

In other places in the world, attention was focused on ethnic groups who were impacted by parallel, complicated political, social and economic events. By 1902, the fighting in South Africa had ended, though the conflict among the British, Dutch and natives continued into the 20th century. As Henry had seen, people in power can complicate the lives of people without power, especially if they are different in some way that is perceived as a threat, or that is not understood.

Jews in Russia knew that as well as anyone. Pogroms—large-scale rioting targeted at Jews—had existed since 1881 when the Jews were accused of the assassination of Tsar Alexander II. Thousands of Jewish homes were destroyed in widespread attacks in the southwestern provinces and many families were reduced to poverty. A series of harsh laws placed on restrictions on Jews, and significant emigration began.

A more violent series of pogroms occurred from 1903–1906, killing 2,000 Jews and wounding many more. The attacks were brutal, and many women and children were slain, surprised in their own homes. Did Henry know about these attacks, and did he ever think about the common fate of many of his own people?

During the years 1902–1910, outside Henry's classroom, America was moving, literally and figuratively. The Wright brothers were finally successful with their airplane on a North Carolina beach in 1903, and a few years later the first Model T was produced. Eventually there would be 15 million sold.

Following a 1905 trip to Japan, Frank Lloyd Wright became celebrated internationally for his Prairie Style of architecture. He would influence thousands of designers all over the world in the years to come.

Oklahoma became the 46th state in 1907, and Arizona and New Mexico followed a few years later. The Indian territories where Reverend Wright, the Roes and others labored were becoming "civilized." The world was coming to America. In 1904, 650 athletes from 12 countries made their way to St. Louis for the Olympic Games. This was the first one held in the United States. This field included the first two black Africans to compete in the Olympics, running the marathon.

American was the land of opportunity, and if there was some prejudice about who might actually be able to take advantage of those opportunities, there were always men and women who defied the odds and were successful in the face of opposition. People in power continued to determine what success was, but during this time there were unexpected individuals who rose to the challenge. Even if Henry Roe Cloud did not know them personally, they were kindred spirits.

Helen Keller was born in Alabama, and when she was 19 months old an illness left her blind and deaf. She and the six year old daughter of the family cook created a crude sign language that allowed her to communicate with her family. At age seven, Helen worked with Anne Sullivan to learn finger spelling, and she eventually learned Braille. In 1904, at the age of 24, Helen became the first blind and deaf person to earn a BA degree when she graduated from Radcliffe College. She had overcome the circumstances of her illness and achieved beyond what anyone imagined was possible for one of the "people without power."

Bobby Jones was born in Atlanta, Georgia and was sick most of his childhood. Who thought that he could develop the strength and stamina to play golf? He learned the game at age six, and won his first tournament that same year, 1908. He went on to become arguably the best golfer in the world.

Jim Thorpe, who was also known by his Indian name Wa-Tho-Huk, was born to parents who were both mixed Native American and European American heritage. He was never a good student and he suffered bouts of depression, especially after the deaths of his twin and his mother. He studied at Carlisle Indian School in Pennsylvania where he was coached by "Pop" Warner and where he was outstanding in every sport he tried, including track and field and football. In 1912 he won the Intercollegiate Ballroom Dancing Championship and the same year he won Olympic gold in Stockholm. Who imagined that a disenfranchised Indian would be hailed around the world?

W.E.B. Dubois grew up the precocious, mixed race son of a poor mother whose health would not allow her to work. He worked odd jobs for money, but he believed that education would improve their lives. His academic gifts allowed him to become the first African American to earn a PhD from Harvard, and in 1909 he helped found the National Association for the Advancement of Colored People, while a professor at Atlanta University.

What factors make a person want to and be able to achieve in the face of adversity? What events in their lives contribute to their drive and their success?

Wo-Na-Xi-Lay-Hunka had journeyed from Winnebago to New Haven. His spiritual journey had taken him from the Medicine Lodge to Christianity. Henry Roe Cloud wanted to be a leader of his people. His loving, adoptive mother constantly told him that leadership was his destiny. As he left Yale, Henry knew that the time was rapidly approaching when his perceived destiny, his wants, and his vision had to take some concrete form if they were to be realized. What he had accomplished to this point could not be the end but only the means.

NOTES

For more information on events in this chapter, consider the following sources:

John Doyle Klier (Editor) and Shlomo Lambroza (Editor), *Pogroms: Anti-Jewish Violence in Modern Russian History* (Cambridge: Cambridge University Press, 2008).

Fred Howard, *Wilbur and Orville: A Biography of the Wright Brothers* (Mineola: Dover Publications, 1998)

Helen Keller, *The Story of My Life: The Restored Classic* (New York: W. W. Norton & Company, 2003)

Bill Crawford, *All American: The Rise and Fall of Jim Thorpe* (Hoboken: Wiley, 2004).

Sally Jenkins, *The Real All Americans: The Team That Changed a Game, a People, a Nation* (New York: Doubleday, 2007).

Chapter Eleven

Oberlin

Henry's determination to make his next trip west "for good" did not turn out that way. He did sell some 80 acres of his land near Winnebago, but his next stop in his educational odyssey was not quite as far west as he would have liked and was certainly not permanent. As the Roes had encouraged earlier, Henry decided to enroll in the theological seminary at Oberlin College in Ohio. It was a logical choice. John Shipherd, a Presbyterian minister, and Philo Stewart founded Oberlin, Ohio, in 1833. Oberlin College was progressive, revivalist, somewhat ecumenical, and had a missionary orientation. It had come into its own with the arrival of the Lane Rebels in 1835. Outraged when the trustees at Lane Seminary tried to curb their antislavery activities, several faculty and students came to Oberlin under the conditions that the college admits students regardless of race and that the seminary be allowed to operate with its inference and regulation. Edward Increase Bosworth was appointed as its first Dean in 1903. Walter Rauschenbusch, who is generally viewed as the father of the Social Gospel in the United States, was a frequent speaker at Oberlin. His belief that Christian ethics should be applied to social problems, like poverty, inequality, alcohol, crime, racial tensions, slums, education, child labor, weak labor unions, and war found a welcome audience there.

Henry began classes at Oberlin on September 22, 1910. The Theological Seminary Bulletin lists him as a member of the junior class.[1] As such his required classes included General Church History, The New Testament, The Ministry, and Homiletics, which is basically defined as the art of preaching. In addition, he could select from a number of electives including music. Henry is also listed as a student in Oberlin's Conservatory of Music. His early thoughts about becoming a musician had long since faded, but his interest and participation in music had not. The Roe's advice to thoroughly immerse himself in campus and community life did not escape Henry. At Oberlin he attended social events such as hayrides, frequently spoke to church and community groups, and dated. He was hired as an assistant minister at Oberlin's First Church where he primarily worked with youth groups but occasionally preached. The small, but regular income from this job certainly helped Henry financially during his studies in Ohio.

It was also during his time at Oberlin that Henry became involved in two organizations that contributed to the mosaic that his life was becoming. While working with the youth ministry, Henry became involved with the Christian Endeavor Society. The Christian Endeavor Society was established in 1881 by Francis E. Clark at the Williston Congregational Church in Portland, Maine. The idea was to give young people both a place and a voice and a place in the work of the church. Clark essentially created the idea of the youth ministry. In 1903 Clark published the Christian Endeavor Manual which he described as a "textbook on the history theory, principles, and practice of the society."[2] The society was based on a pledge although Clark much preferred the word covenant since it implied a two-sided agreement. The elements of that covenant were

> First, I will read the Bible;
> second, I will pray;
> third, I will support my own church;
> fourth, I will attend the weekly prayer meeting of the society;
> fifth, I will take some part in it, aside from the singing;
> sixth, I will perform a special duty at the consecration meeting
> meeting if obliged to be absent.[3]

Unlike the later day bracelet question WWJD?, the question Clark felt that members should ask was "What Would Jesus Have Me Do?" The rest of the manual is a practical guide to setting up the organization for a society. Each section is followed by a set of questions for the reader to answer. The committee structure, constitution, duties of the officers, badges, etc. are described in detail. Like the aforementioned proponents of a social gospel, the Christian Endeavor Society often took positions on controversial issues and advocated direct action—for example, the society gave strong and vocal support to the temperance movement.

It was also at time that Henry became directly involved with the Society of American Indians. From the report of the Executive Council of the first of its annual conferences which was held in Washington, D.C. in 1912, the following account of its creation is given:

> After a correspondence covering a period of more than two years between Professor F. A. McKenzie, of the Ohio State University, Columbus, Ohio, and

a number of representative American Indians, six Indians, Dr. Charles A. Eastman, Dr. Carlos Montezuma, Thomas L. Sloan, Hon. Chas. E. Dagenett, Miss Laura M. Cornelius and Henry Standing Bear, met at Ohio State University on April 3-4, 1911 and started a movement for the organization of a society whose aim should be the highest interests of the race. The movement was given the temporary name of the American Indian Association. During the April meeting the following platform of purposes and policies was adopted as the objects of the new organization:

1st. To promote the good citizenship of the Indians of this country, and to help in all progressive movements of the North American Indians.

2nd. To promote all efforts looking to the advancement of the Indian in enlightenment which makes him free, as a man, to develop according

to the natural laws of social evolution.

3rd. To exercise the right to oppose any movement which appears detrimental to the race.

4th. In all conferences and meeting of this Association, there shall be broad, free discussion of all subjects bearing upon the welfare of the race.

5th. This Association will direct its energies exclusively to general principles and universal interests, and will not allow itself to be used for any personal or private interests. The honor of the race and the good of the country will always be paramount.

6th. It is the sense of the Committee that every member of the Association should exert his influence in every legitimate way to bring before each member of the race the necessity of promoting good citizenship.[4]

Henry Cloud was named to the temporary Executive Committee at the April meeting. The first actual conference of the newly renamed Society of American Indians (SAI) was held at Ohio State University on Columbus Day in 1911. Henry Roe Cloud was present and was a force at that meeting. He was on a panel that discussed religious and moral issues and was named to a committee to draft a statement of purpose. Interestingly, Charles Eastman, who Mary Roe had said Henry would easily eclipse in importance, was on that same committee. The Indian attendees were the most talented, best educated, most creative Native Americans of their generation. The conference is generally viewed as the first real effort at Pan-Indianism of the period. Papers were presented and discussed in a variety of areas including "The Indian in Agriculture," "The Indian as a Skilled Mechanic," "Modern Home-Making and the Indian Woman," "The Philosophy of Indian Education," "The Indian in Art," and "Indians in Professions." Regarding the latter, Henry said

> I like Mr. Oskison's definition of the Indian in the professions. "The man who lives by his wits," and that would include not only the Indians who have gone into the professions such as teaching, the law, medicine, and all that, but

all Indian men and women who have gone out upon their own initiative and worked out their own salvation, perhaps in some line of business. Another speaker has spoken of the fact that the best way to overcome the prejudice that the white man has against us, is to go out in the professions and compete with them, and I want to speak upon this fact. I have noticed among the Indian people a certain prejudice against the Indian who is trying to strike out for himself. Here is an Indian who has started a store, and the Indian passing in the street says, "This man is trying to set himself above me, and I will go and trade with the white man next door," and the white man next door may be the greatest grafter in town, and that Indian who is starting out in business may have had a vision. . .[5]

The conference records are replete with Henry's comments, observations, points of order, and reports. There are also some examples of his wit. In a discussion about Indians and the arts, Charles Doxon said, "I don't suppose we can learn any new line of business, we have got to be satisfied with our own occupation, but some of you have children, and with our children lies the future of the Indian. If you can't train your children, why send them to somebody else who can. If you keep them at your homes, and let them grow up wild and good for nothing, take a tomahawk and scalp yourself. Do all we can to train the young people. I would like to be able to draw, but I have never had patience enough to learn how to make even a decent picture of a horse, but I do think I have the talent for it, if I had only had somebody to take a club and drive me to exercise it. Opportunity is great in all branches of labor. Don't forget that. Take up something and follow that line of work." Henry then replied, "We should congratulate ourselves that there are no tomahawks in this room. You can see how these people have changed their ideas towards one another in the course of the years. I wish that we could make the paleface change his ideas towards us in some such way as the Indians have done one to another."[6] Charles Doxon had written the paper dealing with the Indian as a skilled mechanic. He was a frequent speaker at the Mohonk Conference and was the founder and one of the directors of the Onondaga Indian Welfare Society.

The Society held annual conferences until the 1920's when differences arose among its leaders. The perennial issues of peyote use and the appropriate role of the federal government created many of those differences. Evidence of a developing schism appeared as early as in 1916 when an article in *The American Indian Magazine*, the official publication of the Society said

> The central office of this Society is in constant receipt of letters demanding every sort of thing, from hundred thousand dollar donations to tickets back home for a stranded Indian circus performer. We are asked to indorse books, congressional bills, lawyers, lecturers, patent medicines, tobacco, moving pictures; we are asked to remove Indian superintendents, collect claims, abolish the Indian

Bureau and bring the millennium (sic) to the red race. Because we want to know *why* we should indorse a lecturer or a new brand of catsup we are accused of being prejudiced. Some one has "bought us off," because we cannot fire an Indian agent we do not hire or control or "we are paid by the Indian Bureau to ruin the Indian." We are anxiously awaiting a letter blaming us for the European War. We are blamed by people in the Indian Bureau and by enemies of the Bureau; we are between the millstones constantly. We like to be honestly criticized, for it shows that we *are* doing something and standing for something. It tests our honesty and integrity constantly, and sometimes our patience, but even this is good.

Recently there came a letter accusing our officials of being a "clique" trying to ruin the Indians. We never knew ourselves to be a clique. Perhaps some real clique is after us. At any rate, some one is spreading very disagreeable tales about the officials of the Society. Perhaps this is in accord with the colonial policy of fighting Indians voiced by Col. Washington in 1756. "Unless we can have Indians opposed to Indians," said the Colonel, "we can scarcely expect to succeed against them."[7]

Cloud continued his practice of spending part of the summer with the Roes at Colony and then returning to Winnebago. He made frequent trips back east to speak and addressed crowds as Vassar College in Poughkeepsie, New York, Williams College in Williamstown, Massachusetts, Mount Hermon, and Hampton Institute in Virginia.

Henry was a person both ahead of his time and very much a part of his time. After speaking at Hampton, he wrote, "I leave Hampton for Oberlin at 4 p.m. on the Chesapeake and Ohio. Last night was a wonderful experience for me as I stood and spoke to a thousand negro students, 80 Indians and about two hundred visitors some very distinguished people, on the subject of "character in relation to the personality of Christ." The first twenty minutes was given up to the singing of negro melodies. It stirred my soul. The singing simply carried you off your feet. . . Today before I leave I shall have private meetings with some great big darkies that came forward after the big meeting."

He also met with the young Indian men there and talked with them about "bad women, drinking, need of a great patience on their part, the value of drudgery in study, and their relations with the blacks here."[8] Henry met with the girl students separately and spoke to the Christian Endeavor Society chapter at Hampton.

Another incident took place while Henry was at Oberlin that accentuated the perennial problems of drugs, alcohol, and governmental policies. In one of her letters to him (April 30, 1911), Mary Roe discussed an incident that generated a lot of contemporary and historical interest.[9] They way she described it was that in Santa Fe there was an agent by the name of Crandall who owned and ran a store that sold alcohol. She called it a "booze-selling drug store." The famous prohibitionist William E. "Pussyfoot" Johnson had been actively campaigning among the Pueblos there to try to stop the sale of alcohol to the Indians. Mary indicated that his efforts had been successful and that the Indians were becoming more actively involved and committed. A young Pueblo named Juan Cruz who she described as a "leader for righteousness" attempted to take a bottle of whiskey away from an Indian as he was leaving the saloon. He was then attacked by four or five others and, in an attempt to defend himself, fired a shot "into the darkness." Mary said that "the bullet found and killed a drunken desperado." Cruz was then put in jail by the "liquor men" and was sentenced to be hung. At that point "Pussyfoot" asked the "Indian Department" to provide a defense attorney. Crandall and his associates testified against Cruz, and the Assistant Commissioner Abbott telegraphed "Pussyfoot" that Cruz should be left to his fate. Mary then said that "Pussyfoot" began trying to raise money for Cruz's defense. She felt that this legal atrocity was so great that it might be time to "let loose the dogs of war." Apparently that is what Pussyfoot did by involving the leaders of the Women's Christian Temperance Union which organized a defense committee.

All had not been good between "Pussyfoot" and the government for some time. He had been appointed as a special agent to the Indian Territory and make important enemies. In addition to over 4000 convictions on offenses ranging from gambling to operating and disorderly house, he protested the theft of Indian land by cattle ranchers. If that were not enough, the saloon owners apparently placed a $3,000 bounty on him. Johnson had apparently resorted to usual means to obtain information. He openly admitted that, in the pursuit of evidence, he had drank, gambled, and lied—unusual behavior for a man who gained his nickname by being "stealth-like" in his endeavors. After he had been called back to Washington, DC, and treated poorly, his disagreement with the government became nearly full-scale war. He resigned from his position in September, 1911.

It is rather interesting that Mary urged Henry to not make any judgments until all of the facts were known and ultimately brought even this topic around to his eventual prominence in the area of Indian leadership saying at one point that "it may be you are the only one God can use to this end." She also added that had just read Dr. Eastman's book, *The Soul of the Indian*, and that she did not consider it to be an honest book. She said that Henry would have to write "that book."[10]

From the outset Henry knew that the time he spent at Oberlin would be very limited. There were obvious advantages for him there. The proximity to Columbus made it possible for him to take an active leadership position in the seminal Pan-Indian organization. The intellectual stimulation kept him engaged. The association with the seminary of its Social Gospel orientation kindled his enthusiasm for the ministry. But, in many ways, it was not where he needed or wanted to be. It was not far enough west to be close to Indians—or "his people" as Mary Roe called them. Perhaps, even more importantly at this time, it was too far from the East where he and Walter Roe both knew the greatest opportunities were for raising money. Henry and the Roes had started planning a new endeavor. They were busy trying to arrange support for an Indian school they hoped to begin. They discussed models. Mary Roe and others mentioned Tuskegee. Henry thought about a "Mount Hermon" of the West. His Oberlin experience had been a short but positive one. Slowly he was developing an educational philosophy, and that philosophy evolved significantly over the years. He was making important contacts. His religious beliefs were becoming consolidated. And in the middle of these things, he followed Walter Roe's advice to enroll at Auburn Theological Seminary. In a April 9, 1911 letter to Mary Roe Henry also announced that he planned to enroll in a master's program in ethnology and sociology at Yale (the program was actually called Anthropology and Sociology)—yet another reason to be in the East. He ended that letter by saying "Goodnight Nani. I am embracing you and kissing you in my imagination. Your son."[11]

NOTES

1. *Catalogue of the Oberlin Theological Seminary: 1910—1911,* (Oberlin College, 1911), 11.
2. Rev. Francis Edward Clark, *The Christian Endeavor Manual,* (Boston: United Society of Christian Endeavor, 1903).
3. Clark, *The Christian Endeavor Manual,* 58.
4. "Report of the Executive Council," *First Annual Meeting of the Society of American Indians,* (Washington, D.C.: Society of American Indians, 1912), 7.
5. Ibid., 104.
6. Idib., 90.
7. Arthur C. Parker, editor, *The Quarterly Journal of the Society of the American Indian,* 1916, 15.
8. Henry Roe Cloud to Mary Roe, 3 April 1911, Roe Family Papers, Yale University Library, New Haven, Connecticut.
9. Mary Roe to Henry Roe Cloud, 30 April 1911, Roe Family Papers, Yale University Library, New Haven, Connecticut.
10. Mary Roe to Henry Roe Cloud, 30 April 1911, Roe Family Papers, Yale University Library, New Haven, Connecticut.
11. Henry Roe Cloud to Mary Roe, 9 April 1911, Roe Family Papers, Yale University Library, New Haven, Connecticut.

Chapter Twelve

Auburn Theological Seminary

Henry's choice of Auburn Theological Seminary was not capricious or impulsive. Like Oberlin, Auburn had long been associated with progressive religious theology and missionary zeal. It was established in 1818, and it was associated with the Presbyterian Church. Auburn took justifiable pride in the large number of ministers it prepared for the frontier. However, even after deciding to attend the seminary, Henry still professed to be uncertain about his future. He said, "As one trys (sic) to figure out his career, how baffling in its uncertainty it is, isn't it? But this mystery ahead is what gives us hope and the spirit to attempt the work of life."[1]

When Henry attended seminary there it was located in the city of Auburn, in Cayuga County, New York. The Onondaga Indian Reservation was only 45 miles away, and while it was certainly different from Winnebago, Henry Roe Cloud had to be pleased that a concentration of Native Americans was that close. Perhaps even more attractive in a utilitarian way was the school's location in the East. Henry had long associated good education with the East, and it was fortuitous that Auburn was in New York—close to the people and associations where he and the Roes had successfully raised money. It was also closer to the venues, the colleges and churches, where Henry was developing his reputation as a speaker and was nearing star status. He was also a frequent presenter and participant at the Mohonk Conference Ulster County, New York.

The city of Auburn itself had its own distinctions. It was the hometown of General Abner Doubleday who is recognized as the father of baseball. Harriet Tubman, an escaped slave who served as a Union spy and is more widely known for her work with the underground railroad, a way of helping escaped slaves flee the South, lived in Auburn. William Seward, former Governor of New York, a United States Senator and the United States Secretary of State under Abraham Lincoln and Andrew Johnson is buried in the Fort Hill Cemetery as is Harriet Tubman. Tubman died in 1913, the same year that Henry received his degree from Auburn.

In 1939, the seminary relocated to New York City where it continues to occupy a campus with Union Theological Seminary on Broadway Avenue. Little remains of the original seminary in Auburn except for the Willard Memorial Chapel and the adjoining Welch Memorial Building. The Willard Chapel is the work of Louis C. Tiffany and Tiffany Glass and Decoration Co. and is considered the only complete and unaltered Tiffany chapel known to exist today.

The program of study at Auburn included the Old Testament, Hebrew and Cognate Languages, New Testament including Greek exegesis, Theism and Apologetics, Theology, Homiletics, Sociology, Church History, Practical Theology (including doctrinal and administrative standards of the Presbyterian Church), the English Bible, Religious Education, Music, Elocution, and the study of Christian and non-Christian missions. Despite a formidable course load and work on his master's at Yale, Henry energetically continued to participate in almost all aspects of campus life at the seminary. He continued with his speaking engagements at churches and school in New York and throughout New England. Despite all of these responsibilities, he also worked part-time in the school library to help with his expenses. His letters show that he was almost always in a state of catch-up or even make-up in his school work. On March 8, 1912 he wrote George B. Stewart, President of the seminary, to tell him that he was planning to stay after the term ended for two months just to make up missed work.[2] He received several extensions, and at one point Walter Roe wrote Dr. Stewart to ask for his understanding as Henry did valuable work for "his people"[3]—an expression Henry never used. In that letter Walter admitted that he doubted that Henry would ever be a pastor of a church, but that he was being prepared for a broader Christian leadership. Auburn's records show that Cloud began his work there in December, 1911. He received credit for his work at Oberlin and was awarded 27 credits in many of the courses required at Auburn. That he should even attempt all that he was doing is remarkable. That he should succeed in all he did was even more so. He even took the time to be part of a Winnebago delegation to Washington to petition the government on behalf of tribal members in Wisconsin and Nebraska seeking to extend the period of trust protection the federal government had established. Although he was young and agreed to be part of the delegation while not really knowing the purpose of the trip, Henry apparently acquitted himself well.

The year of 1913 was an eventful one for Cloud. As his graduation from the seminary approached he became increasingly concerned about the things that he might have missed during his frequent and sometimes prolonged absences. In his letters to Mary Roe he talked about how "strenuous"[4] it was, and he expressed concerns about being embarrassed by his performance. He was not only facing examinations in his courses but also oral and written examinations by the Presbytery as he prepared for ordination.

Walter Roe's health had been extremely poor for a long time. However, long bouts with illness did little to limit his commitment and efforts in the mission field. He made frequent long and difficult trips across Indian Country from Colony to the isolated villages of the Mescalero in New Mexico. He journeyed west to California and east to New England in his fund raising endeavors. The situation with the Chiricahua Apache demanded an increasingly large amount of his time. Henry had become involved in their cause as well. Walter's trips to Washington to intercede for them and to petition the government were taking a terrible toll on his health. Finally, on March 12, 1913, while in Nassau, the Bahamas trying to recover and gain a little strength, he died. His death took place less than a week after his 53rd birthday and less than two months before Henry's service of ordination. On May 5, 1913 Henry Roe cloud was ordained a minister of the Presbyterian Church at Willard Memorial Chapel on the Auburn campus. The sermon was delivered by Dr. Charles Gorman Richards who was the minister at the First Presbyterian Church in Auburn.

With his ordination and graduation from Auburn it might seem that Henry's formal education had finally come to an end. However, he was still enrolled in the masters program at Yale. Although several sources indicate that he received his Masters from Yale in 1912, Henry was actually awarded that degree in 1914. In his 1911 letter to the Dean of the Yale Graduate School Henry indicated that he wanted to do the work for the degree over a two period and while not on campus.[5] Yale's absentia rule allowed him to do so. At that time Yale's rules and regulations about advanced degrees were considerably less stringent than they became later. The college bulletin indicated that "such Bachelors of Arts of Yale College as do not find it convenient to take a course of advanced studies in residence may, not less than three years after graduation, be admitted to the degree, upon examination covering a course of study approved in advance by the faculty, or upon submission of a printed essay which shall be deemed adequate evidence of proficiency."[6] So, along with an endorsement from Professor Albert G. Keller, Henry submitted a check for twenty-five dollars and began his master's program in anthropology and sociology. The course requirements for that master's degree normally included classes in anthropology, sociology, Self-Maintenance of Society ("a study, mainly ethnological, of the beginnings of the industrial and governmental organizations. Early development of labor, capital, cooperation, exchange, and property; of war, classes, and social policy."), Self-Perpetuation of Society ("An ethnological and historical study of the marriage institution, the family, and population."), and a class interestingly entitled The Mental Outfit, ("A study, mainly ethnological, of the beginnings and evolution of religion and science. Animism, daimonolgy, shamanism, and their out-reaching and derivations."). Instead of these classes, Henry was assigned an extensive list of books to read. That list included books such as Gregory's *Physical and Commercial Geography,* several books by Charles Graham Sumner and Herbert Spencer, Westrermarck's *History of Human Marriage,* Frazer's *The Golden Bough,* James Elbert Cutler's *Lynch Laws,* and Caleb Williams Saleeby's *Parenthood and Race Culture: An Outline of Eugenics.* That last book, written in 1909, contained the statement that "our primary idea, beyond dispute, is selection for parenthood based upon the facts of heredity. This, however, is not an end, but a means. Some eugenists seem to forget that distinction. Our end is a better race."[7] By the time Henry Cloud had been assigned this book to read, the eugenics movement had caught hold in many scientific circles in the United States and abroad. Nearly two decades before the state of Connecticut has passed a law which forbade the marriage of "epileptics, imbeciles, and feebleminded persons."[8] In 1907, Indiana became the first state to authorize involuntary sterilization of the same group of people.

Henry's performance in his independent study program met the expectations of Dr. Keller who, on May 20, 1914, wrote to the Dean that he recommended him whole-heartedly for the M.A. degree. He said that he had been assigned a great deal of reading, and that Henry had done it and had "thought about it too."[9] He also complimented Henry for several articles that he had written and published in journals like *The Southern Workman.* Furthermore, Keller said that he was aware of the "fine and unremitting work done by Cloud in his efforts in behalf of his race, which include onerous and delicate tasks of all sorts."[10] In June, 1914 Henry was awarded a Masters of Arts from Yale. As was true of his undergraduate graduation, he did not attend the ceremony.

NOTES

1. Henry Roe Cloud to Mary Roe, 12 April 1911, Roe Family Papers, Yale University Library, New Haven, Connecticut.

2. Henry Roe Cloud to George B. Stewart, 3 March 1912, Roe Family Papers, The Archives of the Burke library (Columbia University Libraries) at Union Theological Seminary. New York, New York.

3. Walter Roe to George B. Stewart, 27 February 1912, Roe Family Papers, The Archives of the Burke library (Columbia University Libraries) at Union Theological Seminary. New York, New York.

4. Henry Roe Cloud to Mary Roe, 16 April 1913, Roe Family Papers, Yale University Library, New Haven, Connecticut.

5. Henry Roe Cloud to Dean of the Graduate School, Yale University, 10 March 1911, Roe Family Papers, Yale University Library, New Haven, Connecticut.

6. *Bulletin of Yale University,* (New Haven: Yale University, 1909), 317.

7. Caleb Williams Saleeby, *Parenthood and Race Culture: An Outline of Eugenics,* (New York: Moffat, Yard, and Company, 1909), viii.

8. Robert J. Cynkar, "Buck v. Bell: "Felt Necessities"v. Fundamental Values?," (*Columbia Law Review*, 1981): 1432

9. Dr. Albert G. Keller to Dean Oertel, Yale University, 20 May 1914, Roe Family Papers, Yale University Library, New Haven, Connecticut.

10. Dr. Albert G. Keller to Dean Oertel, Yale University, 20 May 1914, Roe Family Papers, Yale University Library, New Haven, Connecticut.

Chapter Thirteen

The Roe Indian Institute

It is difficult to say precisely when Henry and Walter Roe decided that they were actually going to create a school for Indian youth. The uncertainty of Henry's educational plans before 1910 suggests that it was not before then. However, it is clear that during 1911 they openly communicated and corresponded about "the school." It is known that the idea of a school was presented to representatives at Yale at a time the university was vesting its interests and efforts in China with the Yalu mission. The Y.M.C.A. and the Mohonk Conference endorsed the concept, and Home Missions Council went so far as to appoint a committee made up of the Roes, Thomas C. Moffett, and Dr. C.L. White to begin the preparations for the school in 1912. That special committee met on February 14, 1912. They were joined by Neil McMillian of the Y.M.C.A. and Leila Styles Frissell from the Y.W.C.A. They unanimously agreed that there was a need for a school. They indicated that the objective of such a school would be primarily to prepare Indians for Christian leadership. They also said that the school should be "undenominational and interdenominational" and college preparatory. They went so far, at the Roes' urging, to suggest that Henry Roe Cloud might be the principal.[1]

Until this committee issued its report, it would have been equally difficult to identify precisely what kind of school Roe and Cloud had in mind. In an address at the 28th Annual Meeting of the Mohonk Conference in 1910, Henry seemed to endorse the George Junior Republic School in New York. It was a type of industrial related reformatory concept crated by William Reuben George. The school was designed to replicate the government of the United States as closely as possible in an effort to teach good citizenship and responsibility to neglected or "wayward" children. Henry said, "Why not institute some such a republic among the Indian people? When the bases of education are shifting at the present time, why not start some such an institution among the Indian people, without the stigma of a reformatory school, for the good Indians that are among them and train them to appreciate law and make them intelligent, independent individuals?"[2]

There were at least two things Henry and Walter were sure of from the beginning of their efforts. First, the school would have a strong Christian orientation. To emphasize that point, in April of 1911, Henry wrote Walter that "if we get the school started then we could easily start the Y.M.C.A. having the school as its base of operation."[3] In *From Wigwam to Pulpit*, Henry wrote that "Christian education is the great need of the Indians today."[4] Second, for the school to succeed, financial support and endorsements from noteworthy people, primarily in the East, were necessary.

What had started out as a vision of Walter Roe's became Henry's attempt at creating a memorial to him. According to Henry, they had "only taken the first step" in establishing the school by the time Walter died. Henry then added that his own "life is now committed to the carrying forward of this enterprise."[5] That wholehearted commitment did not diminish the fact that the enterprise was going to be a difficult one to realize. Barely a month after Walter's death, Henry wrote to Mary saying that "I don't really know what I'm to do. I'm totally in the dark. School, missions, trustees, etc."[6] This momentary self-doubt seemed to evaporate rather quickly. By mid-May, Henry was actively trying to enlist other members to the Board of Advisors that Walter and the committee had started strategically building the year before. On May 16, 1913, shortly after he graduated from Auburn, Henry wrote a letter to the President of Auburn, Dr. George B. Stewart. In that letter he said that he wanted to talk with him about the Christian Indian school he intended to start during the upcoming year. He said that one of the first problems he faced in this endeavor was to "get many influential men and women to act as an advisory board for the school." He was asking for the "backing of their names—their influence" and not their financial support. They, and their support, were necessary to win the "confidence and support" of others. He provided Dr. Stewart with a list of prominent people who were serving or would be asked to serve on the board.[7] Among them was Anson Phelps Stokes II, the son of Anson I, the banker and philanthropist and Helen Louisa Phelps. Anson II was an Episcopal priest. Katherine and Eben Olcott were also members. Olcott was President of the Hudson River Day Line and had been a preeminent mining engineer. Dr. Thomas C. Moffitt of the Presbyterian Church Home Mission Board was among the members of the first board. Mary Irick Drexel, the wife of George W. Childs Drexel, was also a member. The Drexels were patrons of the arts as well as philanthropic causes. At one point, she was the head of the Red Cross in Philadelphia. Robert E. Speer, the head of the Presbyterian Board of Foreign Missions is listed as a member as well. Several other dignitaries are mentioned, and many actually served on the board for various amounts of time. Henry listed Mrs. William Borden as a member. The previous month Henry had written Mary Roe that "today's Chicago papers announced the sudden death of Wlm. Borden a young millionaire who had given his life to missionary work among the Mohammedan Chinese. . . Billy died in Cairo, Egypt of spinal meningitis. He was a Yale man '09, member of Elihu Club and a close friend of mine. . . He consecrated his life, his wealth and his all to god's service. . . Billy advised me on a good many of the important steps I took at college."[8] Borden was born into wealth and privilege. His family formed the Borden Dairy company. For a high school graduation gift, he was given a trip around the world and on that trip discovered his calling. He was moved by the hurt he saw among the world's poor. At Yale he was president of a very large and active missionary group and was also President of Phi Beta Kappa. Despite obvious differences in background, Borden and Henry shared many common traits, and Henry was obviously affected by his death. Another prominent member was John R. Mott. Mott, who won the Nobel Peace Prize in 1946, led the Y.M.C.A. The noted theology professor at Vassar and author of the widely read *Introduction to the Life of Christ*, Dr. William Bancroft Hill, participated both in terms of being on the advisory board and being a substantial financial supporter. With the approval and support of the Home Missions Council of New York City in 1914, it became obvious that the school, now generally referred to as the Roe Indian Institute, was indeed going to become a reality. There remained just a few unanswered questions. What kind of school would it be? Where would it be located? How would it be sustained?

A simple answer to that first question was—not the kind of school Henry had attended at Genoa, Winnebago, or Santee. What he and Roe came to envision was a college preparatory secondary school for Native Americans. To completely understand the scope of that challenge, one must readjust his or her historical lens. By the turn of the twentieth century there were slightly over 6000 public high schools in the United States. Before the Kalamazoo case in 1875 the legality of a publicly funded college preparatory high school was questionable. With the increase in the number of high schools, the questions of standardization of curriculum and purpose arose. There were significant competing academic philosophies that needed to be resolved. One philosophy favored ideas like rote memorization, and another favored critical thinking. One philosophy viewed American high schools as institutions that should and would from the start divide students into college-bound and working-trades groups. Often that distinction was based on race or ethnicity. Another perspective was to provide a standardized course of study for all students. One philosophy promoted classic studies, including Greek and Latin, while the opposing other view stressed practical studies. The N.E.A. (National Education Association) attempted to address these issues when they appointed the Committee of Ten in 1892. The Committee recommended twelve years of education for all students, with eight years of elementary education to be followed by four years of high school. It was further recommended that all students would be taught, regardless of their further education plans or careers. There was a strong implication in their work that high school should have an inherently strong college preparatory function. Despite this and other efforts while Henry Cloud and Walter Roe were planning and raising money for their college preparatory Indian school, only about six or seven percent of the teenage population finished high school and probably fewer than one third of those actually went to college.

Four years after he addressed the Lake Mohonk Conference and extolled the virtues of the George Junior Republic School, Henry returned specifically to talk about education. Unlike in his 1910 speech, which was a subject of much discussion because he advocated that Indians be taxed as a way of promoting responsibility, he gave more details and insight as to what the Roe Indian Institute might look like. He talked about the importance of education for a complete life. He talked about a holistic approach involving "heart, head, and hand." He commented at length about the inadequacies of educational opportunities within the homes of most Indians and the lack of educational values. He used the expression "race inertia" regarding meaningful and responsible work. He addressed the issue of leadership among the Indians by saying

> The first effort, it seems to me, should be to give as many Indians as are able, all the education that the problems they face clearly indicate they should have. This means all the education the grammar schools, the secondary schools, and the colleges of the land can give them. This is not any too much for the final equipment of the leaders of the race. If we are to have leaders who will supply disciplined mental power in our race development they cannot be merely grammar-school men. They must be trained to grapple with these economic, educational, political, religious, and social problems. They must be men who will take up the righteous cause among their people, interpret civilization to their people, and restore race confidence, race virility. Only by such leaders can race segregation be overcome. Real segregation of the Indian consists in segregation of thought and inequality of education. We would not be so foolish as to demand a college education for every Indian child in the land, irrespective of mental powers and dominant vocational interests; but, on the other hand, we do not want to make the mistake of advocating a system of education adapted only to the average Indian child. . . For the Indian of exceptional ability, who wishes to lay his hands upon the more serious problems of our race, the industrial work, however valuable in itself, necessarily retards

him in the grammar school until he is man-grown. He cannot afford to wait until he is twenty-five to enter the high school... Others before me, such as Dr. Walter C. Roe, have dreamed of founding a Christian, educational institution for developing strong, native, Christian leadership for the Indians of the United States. I, too, have dreamed.[9]

In that address Cloud echoes many of the ideas expressed by W.E.B. Dubois a decade before when, in talking about the "talented tenth," said:

The Negro race, like all races, is going to be saved by its exceptional men. The problem of education, then, among Negroes must first of all deal with the Talented Tenth; it is the problem of developing the Best of this race that they may guide the Mass away from the contamination and death of the Worst, in their own and other races. Now the training of men is a difficult and intricate task. Its technique is a matter for educational experts, but its object is for the vision of seers. If we make money the object of man-training, we shall develop money-makers but not necessarily men; if we make technical skill the object of education, we may possess artisans but not, in nature, men. Men we shall have only as we make manhood the object of the work of the schools—intelligence, broad sympathy, knowledge of the world that was and is, and of the relation of men to it—this is the curriculum of that Higher Education which must underlie true life. On this foundation we may build bread winning, skill of hand and quickness of brain, with never a fear lest the child and man mistake the means of living for the object of life.[10]

What the purpose of the school was to be should be a barometer of the pedagogy that guided it. While it might be easy to simply lump Cloud into a group of educators and philosophers called Progressives, it would be extremely short sighted to do so. Both John Dewey and Henry Roe Cloud saw the school as being society-centered. They both saw the limitations of education that was vocationally oriented or focused. But they seem to differ in other significant ways. Dewey is often quoted as saying, "Education is, not a preparation for life; education is life itself." Cloud would take a far more utilitarian approach. Perhaps the biggest difference between the two is in the emphasis the Roe Institute placed on religious training—albeit non-denominational. Henry unapologetically included the phrase "Christian education" in virtually every description of the school, and even referred to the Bible course as the heart of the curriculum. Dewey, on the other hand, encouraged secular inquiry and problem solving. He said that "there is a difference between religion, a religion, and the religious."[11] This is not a distinction Cloud would make. There was at least some interest in the educational approach that "progressives" were following. A November 15, 1928 letter from Cloud to The Progressive Education Association contained seventy-five cents in stamps for a copy of the October–December, 1928 issue of *Progressive Education*.[12]

In 1914 Henry Cloud was asked by Dr. Fayette Avery McKenzie of Ohio State University, a white professor of economics and sociology, to assist him in surveying conditions in Indian schools. McKenzie had been one of the initial founders of the Society of American Indians and was better known than Cloud largely because of his work with the S.I.A. He also had a solid reputation as an academic as a result of his publication of "The Assimilation of the American Indian" and "The Indian in Relation to the White Population of the Unites States." The survey was funded by the Phelps-Stokes Fund. The report itself was concluded in 1915 and seemed to be of marginal, if not negligible, impact at the time. It was largely ignored in the press and was not even mentioned in the Phelps-Stokes Fund Report about educational adaptations, *Educational Adaptations: Report of Ten Years' Work of the Phelps-Stokes Fund, 1910–1920*, and *The Twenty-five Year report of the Phelps Stokes Fund*. McKenzie himself essentially summarized his perceptions of the Indian educational system in 1914, a year before the survey's conclusion, in an article in the *Indian Quarterly*. He said, "The situation with regard to education is very similar. The expenditures for Indian schools as compared with the general Indian budget has increased from one-half of 1 per cent in 1877 to 26.9 per cent. I believe that this proportion should continue to increase. Of the 88,000 Indian youth, 50,000 or 56.3 per cent are today found in some school. Of the children between ten and fourteen years of age, 71.4 per cent are in school; 71.2 per cent of all Indians can speak some English, and 45.4 per cent can read and write to some extent. The ability of the youth to speak English rises to 84.2 per cent and ability to read and write rises to 77.2 per cent. I consider it a great achievement to have effected so completer an introduction to the educational system of our civilization. But we must in all honesty recognize that it is for the great mass of Indians just an introduction. . . It is our rule to require the youth to go to school until they are eighteen, and not infrequently they continue in school until they are twenty-five or more, and yet the most advanced government school is a grammar school. The great mass of the children get very much less. No attempt is made here to appraise the industrial training given in the Indian schools. My object is simply to reveal the inadequacy of the schooling to prepare the Indian for successful competition in the world of business affairs and for a genuine participation in the thought and aspirations of our civilization."[13] The ultimate value of the work of Cloud and McKenzie was not actually realized until 1928 with the publication of the Meriam Report. Many of their findings and recommendations are found there. Of more immediate value to Henry was that he was receiving a salary of $3,000 for traveling around and being able to not only gather information about what he should not do at his school but also to recruit potential students for that same school. In subsequent years Henry's star continued to rise while McKenzie was ultimately forced out of the presidency at Fisk by African-American activists and students who resented his authoritarian and paternalistic treatment of the students there.

The periodic trips Henry made back to Winnebago after 1907 had to show him how atypical his life was from that of "his people." Perhaps so much so that he never used that expression. He referred to "the Indian." In 1914 alone he did things and went places that were beyond the wildest dreams of most other Native Americans at the time. His work with the Phelps Stokes Fund coupled with his speaking engagements and conference meetings probably made him the most widely traveled Indian with a purpose since Tecumseh.

The Society of American Indians held its fourth annual conference in Madison, Wisconsin on October 6—11, 1914. Henry was, of course, in attendance and a prominent figure there. Dr. McKenzie had just returned from a prolonged stay Europe where he was doing "certain sociological studies."[14] Again, the survey of Indian schools could not have been a pressing issue for him at that time. The Executive Committee, including Henry, was re-elected and it seems that most of the business that was done there was of an administrative or organizational nature. It was reported that between 50 and 60 Indians attended along with many associate or non-Indian members. One of the significant things that was accomplished was the naming of a commission that would carry a petition directly to President Wilson. Expectedly, Henry Roe Cloud was named as a member. It was also at that conference that Henry met Elizabeth Bender. Elizabeth was born on the White Earth Reservation in Minnesota in the late nineteenth century. She was sent to the Hampton Institute in Virginia in 1903. After she graduated from Hampton she decided to stay there for post-baccalaureate work. Elizabeth also was somewhat of a celebrity. She was the sister of Charles Albert Bender a well-know major league baseball pitcher. Like most of the Indian athletes of his day, Charles Bender quickly became know through the press as "Chief." He pitched for several years for Connie Mack's Philadelphia Athletics. His career statistics were so impressive that he was admitted to the baseball hall of fame in 1953. Some credit him with developing the slider. Bender was commonly regarded as an intelligent, energetic, hard-working person—characteristics that his sister shared.

Henry was certainly not naïve in terms of relationships with women. He had dated frequently through his time in school, and his travels, no doubt, brought him into frequent contact with interesting, intelligent, and attractive women. He was a handsome, interesting man. However, to this point in his life his primary love interest had been Mary Roe. It was she who had advised and supported him through his dark times. It was her professions of love that bolstered his confidence. It was her visions of his glorious future and calling that challenged and motivated him. After Walter's death, the Missions Board named Mary a "missionary at large," and her interests and involvement with the school continued for several years. Eventually her primary interests in the mission area gradually shifted to Central and South America.

Elizabeth Bender would bring something to the partnership and to the school that Walter, Mary, and Henry did not possess—experience in teaching. In fact, the only real information about the nature of the day-to-day academic experiences of the teachers and students comes from her letters—not Henry's. In 1908 she was sent to Montana to teach at a government school among the Blackfeet. She taught boys and girls ranging from five to fifteen years of age. She had to serve as a house matron for a while and was even know to cook for the students. She treated children with trachoma which is a chronic contagious bacterial conjunctivitis that frequently resulted in blindness if it was not treated. Later that year she was moved to the Ft. Belknap Reservation, also in Montana, where similar problems existed. She administered bluestone (copper sulfate) to almost all of the students in the school. In fact, the condition was so bad there that it was referred to as the "one-eyed reservation."[15] A hundred years later, trachoma still blinds thousands and affects million more in places like Ethiopia. The Carter Center, Lions Clubs International, the Conrad N. Hilton Foundation, and the International Trachoma Initiative have been fighting trachoma in Africa since 1998. Bender was a pioneer in this effort. She taught at several government schools before returning to Hampton for more study in home economics. She also taught at Carlisle Indian School after leaving Hampton in 1915.

Elizabeth confessed that she was smitten with Henry from their first meeting, and the feeling seems to have been mutual. In 1916 they were married, and Henry's contacts with Mary became more typical of that of between a mother and son. They corresponded frequently about school business; she wrote most of her letters address to both Henry and Elizabeth; she inquired about their children; and sent presents. From Madison and the S.A.I. Conference, Henry went on to Lake Mohonk and then to Washington to meet with the President. A little before noon p.m. on December 10, 1914, a 40 person delegation of members of the S.A.I., associate members, and supporters walked into the White House to present President Woodrow Wilson with a "memorial" that had been drafted by a committee formed at their conference in October. The committee was made up of Dennison Wheelock, Hiram Chase, F.A. McKenzie, William J. Kershaw, and Henry Roe Cloud. Wheelock was an Oneida lawyer who was better known as a composer and bandleader; Hiram Chase, also an attorney, was a Omaha Indian; McKenzie was a white sociologist; Kershaw was an attorney from Wisconsin and was Menominee; Cloud was a Presbyterian minister who listed his home as Colony, Oklahoma. Arthur Parker said that "the tenth day of December, nineteen hundred and fourteen, marked a new beginning in Indian progress and proclaimed a new day for the red race." Their petition essentially called for a clear definition of legal status for the Indian and that all claims Indians might have against the United States be heard in the Court of Claims. Parker also said that the President admitted that he "had not given special thought to the Indian, though he had appointed the best man he could find as Secretary of the Interior (Franklin Lane) and as Commissioner of Indian Affairs (Cato Sells)." The delegation received assurances from the President that he would give serious consideration to their memorial, and they left the office to face a "battery of cameras and moving picture machines."[16] They left the White House feeling optimistic and buoyed. They carried that enthusiasm back to the hotel and continued talking formally and informally through the night.

The evening banquet was the culminating event for the occasion. Cato Sells, the Commissioner of Indian Affairs, was the featured speaker; Henry Cloud spoke on the topic of "Brains and Efficiency." Interestingly, this expression was one that President Wilson used in speeches and writings that addressed corporate competition and monopolies. Wilson said, "If they (corporations) can economize their processes and concentrate their energy so that by brains and efficiency they can beat anybody else, I will take my hat off to them as an American."[17] Cloud was applying the same principal to Indian and white relationships. Clearly, education was not far from his mind at any time.

An interesting and somewhat telling complication arose at the banquet. Although it had been hurriedly put together, there was an interest in making it an event commensurate with the occasion. Banquet "favors" had been ordered. Apparently the supplier of those favors, the New York Indian Exhibits Company, did not have the requested miniature peace pipes and sent small war clubs instead—hardly the sentiment the Indians had in mind. So, some quick thinking organizer wrote a poem to wrap around the war clubs. The poem said,

> The Peace Club
> To knock with club and thrust with spear
> Robs life of all its peace and cheer.
> So let us CLUB together, friend,-
> Then our woes shall be at end.[18]

With a bolstered reputation, new potential supporters, and with the addition of a person who was going to be a new partner in his efforts, Henry Cloud began to address some remaining questions about the school. Principal among these was where to locate it. Walter and Henry had discussed various options. They agreed that it should be in the Midwest. The special committee had suggested Santee, Nebraska, the Winnebago reservation, and the Bacone Institute at Muskogee, Oklahoma. Later, Henry reported on possible sites at the Walden College in McPherson, Kansas, Independence, Missouri, Topeka, Kansas, two different sites in Lawrence, Kansas, and the Park College site which was about twelve miles out of Kansas City. They had to consider things like existing facilities, sanitation, climate, and transportation. In the end, all of these factors were considered, but the determining factor may well have been one simple fact—the businessmen and citizens of Wichita, Kansas seemed to want the school. In fact, they openly recruited it.

The local Wichita media chronicled the creation of the school thoroughly and positively. The headline of the *Wichita Eagle* on December 27, 1914 proclaimed "Wichita to Get Indian School," and that it was "backed by rich men."[19] The support of wealthy business and well-known philanthropists was almost as significant as was the fact that the school was to be headed by an Indian, and it was not just any Indian. Henry Cloud was referred to as the "best educated Indian in the United States."[20] According to the newspaper account, Wichita was selected as the site of the school, the only one of its kind (Indian led) in the country "because of its educational atmosphere, the railroad facilities, its moral elements, its proximity to Oklahoma where many of the students will come from, and because of its geographical location near the center of the United States." It was also reported that the site had to be located on a hill because "Indians insist upon being situated on a hill." The story included the information that the school would begin its operation with $5000.00 in its treasury and an additional $50,000 pledged to build buildings and buy more land. G.E.E. (Elmer) Lindquist, a longtime friend of Henry's and the Y.M.C.A. director at Haskell was named the first principal. Although the exact enrollment projections were not known "a number of Indian boys" had said they were going to attend.[21]

An editorial cartoon in the *Wichita Eagle* of December 29, 1914 showed a feather with the words "Indian School" inscribed on it being placed in the hat of a proud looking gentleman along side of other feathers with the names of local schools and colleges like the high school, music schools, Fairmount, Mount Carmel, and the Friend's University.[22] The January 13, 1915 edition of the same newspaper had a story with a headline that read "Showing They Want School," and reported that a committee made up of several businessmen "called on a few citizens" for donations. Wichita's lock on the Indian school suddenly seemed to be in jeopardy, and the next Friday the newspaper reported that "When Danger of Losing Indian Academy is Known Boosters Show Up." This meeting was spearheaded by realtors who were interested in securing money and donating land. A.A. Hyde. The President of the Mentholatum Company attended that meeting. However, by July 4, 1915 the purchase of the land had been finalized, and the trustees of the school gave B.W. McGinnis $10,000 for forty acres. The citizens of Wichita pledged an additional $5,000 and had raised all but $1,700 of that amount. The school would begin operation in the fall, but there were still some lingering questions. Was Henry Roe Cloud the "Booker T. Washington" of his people, like the newspapers said, or was he more like W.E.B. Dubois? Did being the "best educated Indian" in America necessarily equip him to be an effective administrator? Was the Roe Indian Institute going to flourish and turn Wichita, Kansas into a Lake Mohonk? Was the school going to be the "Mount Hermon of the West," or was it going to struggle and even die as the country moved closer to world war, experienced a devastating flu epidemic, and eventually slipped into an economic depression?

In a January 31, 1914 letter to Dr. H.B. Frissell, Henry said that "my life is financed, and my time will be given to the financial end of the work (of the operation of the school), and I sincerely hope that there will never be a serious financial burden upon the trustees."[23] However, by 1923, his perspective had changed. In one of many letters to E.E. Olcott, Henry said that "the fact of the matter is if the trustees are going to put the whole load on me this institute is doomed to fall down... The Board of Trustees of Hampton Institute raises all the money now for the Principal of Hampton Institute. The Board of Trustees raise all of the money for the Principal of Mount Hermon."[24] From its inception to the day he left the school, such was not to be the case at Roe Institute. He was always involved in fundraising, and not always to the satisfaction of the Board of Trustees. His annual reports to the Board include very little about anything other than finances, building, and property acquisitions. He does often talk about the history of Christian education among the Indians and quotes from Dr. A.L. Riggs, his former mentor when he said that "it is evident that Protestant missions must get a new grip on these Indian people to accomplish their Christianization. A fundamental lack is the absence of training. Schools are a necessity but they are totally wanting or too weak."[25] His remarks about the school, in the reports and in letters about the school are generally positive but vague—statements like "the school work is going on very nicely;" "our school is opening up most auspiciously;" "the school was never better than it was today."[26]

The Roe Indian Institute began operation with eight students, and actually only six had classes as part of the school. The other two went to the local public school. *The Southern Workman* acknowledged the opening by saying that it "quietly opened its doors at Wichita, Kansas, with a handful of students and a few instructors, and has made a modest beginning under the leadership of

Henry Roe Cloud."[27] The students were charged $150.00 per year. But these costs were considered operating costs intended to be used to pay for food, lodging, etc. Scholarships from benefactors were given to defray the costs. The students had to work two hours each day to accumulate work credit for his account. During its first year of operation the school had to delay construction of a permanent building and instead used what was called a "war emergency hut." The school owned sixty acres and land for cultivation and rented an additional twenty-five. The first financial report of the school showed total receipts of $32,197.19 Real estates, livestock, machinery, and other capital assets totaled over $17,000. The school had a cash balance of nearly $4,000 and had established a new building reserve which carried a $2,816 balance. The purchase of property accounted for more over $7,000 of the disbursements while school operating expenses accounted for slightly more than $7,000. Henry's salary of $1,200 was paid by a person (A.T. VanSantvoord) identified in budgetary reports as a "friend of the Institute."[28] Substantial contributions to the school also came from Mary Roe, and even Henry occasionally loaned money to the school. One interesting donation that was recorded was in the amount of $1.00 given to Mrs. Roe by "some lady." Detailed lists of the contributors to school reveal considerable local support from Wichita as well as prominent business men and philanthropists from New York, Washington D.C., etc. The estimated budget for the first year had been projected to be $27,800.00, and Henry indicated that a minimum of $30,000 was necessary to begin operations. By this measure, the school got off to a successful start. However, Henry and the Trustees were always desirous of one or two big donations from people like the McCormicks or Rockefellers and the impact those could have on the school fund raising efforts. The Daughters of the American Revolution and the Phelps-Stokes Fund were consistent supporters.

Eben E. Olcott of the Hudson River Day Line served as Treasurer for the Board of Trustees, and his admonitions to Henry that he raise more money range from indirect and subtle to desperate. Olcott and Dr. William Bancroff Hill urged Henry to intensify his fundraising efforts with the Indian population. On January 13, 1923, Olcott wrote to Henry during the last Board meeting, "the greatest emphasis was laid upon your raising considerably more money, both in the East and West, or at least doing all we possibly can in this direction."[29] He sometimes sent Cloud pamphlets and fundraising materials from organizations that he thought were doing a good job raising money. Te Institute published brochures with titles like "Significance of the American Indian Institute in Indian Affairs,"[30] "Why Should I Help the American Indian Institute," and "A Challenge to Christian America" that featured a picture of a young Harry Coons in traditional Pawnee dress as well as one taken later of him in his military uniform. It contained the caption, "American Indian Institute Makes Christian Citizens." Henry responded to Olcott's urgings in April, 1923 by saying that "I beg of you to be patient for we are moving irresistibly toward good definite results financially."[31] In May he wrote that it "is very difficult to get contributions from among the Indians."[32] Olcott, although a close friend of Henry's, occasionally seemed to lose patience with him. In January, 1924 he wrote to Henry that "at the Annual Meeting, Dr. Hill repeated his request that we should note every cent coming to the Institute from you and every cent expended to run the Institute. We have written about this over and over again. Please see this is done absolutely." Then, in his own handwriting, he added, "We want our every move to be fine and uplifting."[33] In what was more of a marketing decision than a change in philosophy, the Board of Trustees, at its January 1919 meeting voted to change the name of the Roe Indian Institute to the American Indian Institute. While Henry had been intent to honor Walter Roe by naming the Institute after him, it became apparent that the school was losing potential financial support by being too closely associated with the Reformed Church. Even Mary Roe acknowledged the need to change its name. It was questionable that Walter Roe would have even favored the school's initial name anyway.

In 1923, Henry Cloud was named as a member of the Secretary of the Interior Hubert Work's Committee of One Hundred. In September, Henry called the effort "the one bright and hopeful undertaking for the Indians just at the present time."[34] The committee was made up of an eclectic group of Indians and non-Indians. The committee met in Washington on December 12 and 13, 1923. Actually, only about sixty of those invited actually came. The accomplishments of the committee are subject to debate. The recommendations did have some impact of the Miriam Report, and the next year President Coolidge did sign the Indian Citizen Act. The next day Henry wrote to Mr. Olcott that "great constructive measurers were put up to the Secretary of the Interior affecting the welfare of the Indians," and that General Hugh Scott had stood up to say that he was a trustee of the Institute and that he hoped that the government would extent scholarship assistance to Indians going to school there.[35] Scott had only recently been named to the Board of Trustees, and Cloud no doubt felt it was important to tell Olcott about the school's mention in a national forum.

By 1925, Olcott's concerns about finances had only increased. A $25,000 pledge from Ernest Thompson had been tied up and eventually killed in the Department of the Interior because it involved money that came from a person on the Pawnee reservation, and there was current litigation in the courts about Indian donations. An anticipated $5,000 from Cyrus McCormick had been reduced to $250.00. On October 3, 1925, Olcott wrote to Henry, "What are we going to do? We have again sent you the full amount for October 1st, but we have heard nothing from you in reference to the appeal that we have sent on for your best effort and we can not get along this way. Why do you not answer our direct, urgent, and vital questions? I am almost desperate. I do not want to fail but what am I to do?"[36]

It was becoming obvious that some change needed to be made. In December Henry wrote to Dr. Hill that the school needed to become a joint project between the Dutch Reformed Church and the Presbyterian Church in the U.S.A. Both had dealt with Indian issues in the past. Dr. Hill's response was not encouraging, although he did tell Henry that it was sometimes "darkest just before the dawn."[37] By the end of 1926, it was evident that the Board of National Missions of the Presbyterian Church was willing to take over the operation of the school. On March 22, 1927 Edna Voss informed Cloud that, acting on the recommendation of both the Advisory Board of the Division of Schools and Hospitals and the Staff Council of the Board of National Missions of the Presbyterian Church in the U.S.A., the Board had agreed to take over the Institute.[38] Henry's role in fundraising and finances was far from over. Full financial control would not be given to the Board for three years, and the school had to continue operating. Also, the school was not subjected to another level of bureaucracy, and it was one that required even more than the Board of Trustees. In October of 1927, Henry received a letter from Anna M. Scott Assistant Secretary of the Missions Board that detailed some of those accountability expectations. The Board expected a monthly statistical report, a statement about how the students were getting along, improvements that had been made, and a monthly report to the Synodical executive.[39]

In February, 1928 the office secretary wrote to Henry that the annual report had not been received and that the requisitions, report on workers, and staff report had not been receive either.[40] The secretary, Florence Goddard, wrote again in March to say that they had not received the per capita cost questionnaire, and that she trusted "that you have not forgotten about" it.[41] In June she reminded him to send ion the vouchers included in the monthly financial statement. The Secretary, Edna Voss corresponded frequently with Henry as well. In August, she told him that they did not have evidence that the Institute was developing some system of keeping up with its former students.[42] In September she noted that an inventory report due on July 15 had not been received by September 12. In December 1929, the office reminded Henry that the fire drill questionnaire had not been received.[43]

By the end of 1930, Henry Cloud's salary had reached $3,000. He was sometimes, depending of the length of his absences from the Institute, called president, or principal, or superintendent. In 1932, the Board approved not only an "additional six percent cut, but voted another even larger one. I feel that this very definitely means that the institute will have to run next year on a smaller budget than that which we have provided the present year."[44] By the end of the decade, there could be no question that Henry Roe Cloud had achieved the position of being one of, if not the most, influential Native American in the United States, but there could also be no question that the headaches and concerns about operating the Institute were not going to go away or even get any smaller.

In 1931, the Commissioner of Indian Affairs, Charles J. Rhoads, offered Cloud a position in the Indian Office in Washington. Henry was obviously tired of the fundraising and the constant pressure that went along with it. Even though it meant, in essence, "going over to the enemy," Cloud quickly accepted the offer. He was given a leave of absence from the Institute and went to Washington against the advice of members of the Board of Home Missions. Even this decision proved to be more problematic than Cloud could have anticipated. In addition to the criticism from people he had been working with for several years, he did not pass the Civil Service examination required for the new job. The "best educated Indian in the nation" had failed the test. This revelation could do a couple of disastrous things. First, after the highly touted appointment, Cloud now could face public humiliation. Second, the Indian Office itself, and the Civil Service Office faced criticism. Native American advocates had, for years, been calling for more Indians to be appointed to higher positions in the government. What was there about the selection criteria and the exam itself that prevented that from happening? Eventually the situation was remedied by appointing Cloud to a position that did not require the exam. He was made a type of roving field investigator who focused on Indian education. It had become obvious that Henry Cloud was no longer going to be involved with the Institute. He urged the Home Missions Board to make his wife, Elizabeth, head of the school. The choice made sense. She had been at the school from the beginning. She knew almost everything that needed to be known about its operation. She had been involved with every aspect of it. In fact, during Henry's frequent absences, she was in essence in charge. However, citing a rule that prohibited women from heading schools where adolescent boys were being served, the Board refused his request. Henry Roe Cloud resigned from the Institute late in 1932. Elizabeth followed with her resignation in September of 1934.

It is difficult to determine the actual success of the Institute in terms of educational value added for the students. The overarching emphasis on what Cloud called "Christian leadership" obscures any real examination of the academic successes or failures of the school. Early administrators like Cloud, Gustavus (Elmer) Emanuel Lindquist, A.B. Tenney, and Huber Burr were missionary oriented and concerned more with saving souls that broadening minds.

Both Lindquist and Burr achieved notoriety in the mission field. No effective follow-up reporting system existed at that time, and success in college was impossible to obtain any way other than anecdotally. Early subject area teachers seemed to be well-grounded in content if not pedagogy. Mrs. Lucie Hoare was the wife of Dr. A.J. Hoare who was on the faculty at Fairmont College. He was active in leadership positions in the Mathematics Association of America. Students at Fairmont College like Lester Wilkinson, Laura Smith, Shirley Smith, and Dorothy Dymock frequently taught academic courses. Elizabeth Bender Cloud took an active part in the instructional program. She frequently communicated directly and indirectly with the parents of students at the Institute. She wrote to Mary Roe that the students "have just finished their semester examinations and as far as I have been able to learn, most of them have passed and some of them with very good grades. Tell Jimmy Downs (in Colony, Oklahoma) that his son is certainly winning a place for himself here. I notice that Robert is in need of shoes very much and a new pair of trousers. If Mr. Downs could spare about $12.00 and send it to me, I would see to it that Robert got the things he needed. John Washee continues to be steady and dependable. Joel is gradually getting over his mental trouble I think. We do not push him too hard in his school work."[45] This selection reveals two significant things. It is obvious that many of the students at the Institute were from the area around Colony where the Roes had been so important for many years. It is also clear that Elizabeth took a great deal of interest in the students and that she was a careful observer of their condition. She described the teachers at the Institute as a "loyal group of teachers who are cooperating with us in every way."[46] She said that as lead teacher it was Lucie Hoare's responsibility to construct the school's schedule and to "see that we follow strictly the course of study as outlined by the state of Kansas. The school was on the Kansas list of accredited schools.

In 1928, Dawn Tulley completed the High School Principal's Report for the Institute that was required from the State of Kansas Department of Education.[47] She indicated that there were four full-time teachers and 38 students. (By 1930, there were 49 students.) Classes were forty minutes long, and 15 units were required for graduation. A grade of 70 was considered passing for each course. The previous year's graduating class had five students, and two of them were attending college. One other was attending a commercial school. The other two were receiving more high school study. Other questions included such things as how large were the school grounds; how are internal walls finished; is the heating system satisfactory; what is the source of the water supply, what methods of cleaning were used for the toilets (rubbing and chemicals); how are the laboratories equipped; what is the number of volumes in the library (2500)? All of the teachers had A.B. degrees and were from the states of Iowa, Pennsylvania, Missouri, and Kansas. Dawn

Tullis taught English and American history. A.W. Barber taught Biology, General Science, Constitution, and Physics. Anne Griffith taught Algebra, Geometry, and History. Eunice Craig taught Spanish and English. The curriculum was unremarkable, but there were electives offered in the areas of Solid Geometry, Advanced American History, Civics, and Sociology. In the space provided for the principal to describe additions or changes Dawn had written that they had acquired one new teacher's desk and three and one-half dozen arm chairs.

There was one aspect of the total school program that Henry not only supported but spearheaded—the incorporation of Indian culture. This was contrary to the position he had taken earlier and was in stark contrast to most of the other Indian schools, governmental and private, that were still trying to "kill the Indian" by removing all vestiges of his/her culture. Henry Cloud had seemingly advocated assimilation, but at the Institute the students celebrated "Indian Days" that emphasized traditional dances, art, and games. He also allowed students to retain and use their Indian names. The school's newspaper, *The Indian Outlook,* was Henry primary way of advancing his opinions as well as the accomplishments of the school. Despite the fact that his administrative responsibilities, primarily fundraising, precluded his participating as an active classroom teacher, he did maintain a degree of involvement that allowed him to gain a national reputation as an educator. In that sense his rise to prominence in that field was not at all unlike that of politicians who have become "the education governor," "the education president," or even presidents of universities and heads of schools and school systems. Because of his personal story and education and his involvement with the Institute, Henry Roe Cloud had become the "education Indian." Interests and support of the Institute waned after he left, and the school closed in 1939. There had been some doubters and distracters—some prominent and some not. Richard Henry Pratt of Carlisle fame, or infamy, thought that the approach was all wrong. Henry dismissed him as a bitter old man. Some students were as unhappy at the Institute as Henry had been at the government schools. Some did not return from breaks and vacations, and some just walked away. However, for the most part, the people who came in contact with Wo-Na-Xi-Lay-Hunka as a youth, Henry Clarence Cloud as a young adult, and Henry Roe Cloud as an adult wanted him to succeed, and he certainly did that.

NOTES

1. Minutes, Meeting of Special Committee, 14 February 1912, Records of the American Indian Institute, 1908–1954, PCUSA Board of National Missions, West Lafayette.

Chapter Thirteen

2. Henry Roe Cloud,"The Indian's Relation to the Community," *The Twenty-Eighth Annual Lake Mohonk Conference,* (Lake Mohonk: Lake Mohonk Conference, 1910), 14–16.

3. Henry Roe Cloud to Walter Roe, 21 April 1911, Roe Family Papers, Yale University Library, New Haven, Connecticut.

4. Henry Roe Cloud, "From Wigwam to Pulpit," *Missionary Review of the World*, (May 1915): 15.

5. Cloud, "From Wigwam to Pulpit," 15.

6. Henry Roe Cloud to Mary Roe, 22 April 1913, Roe Family Papers, Yale University Library, New Haven, Connecticut.

7. Henry Roe Cloud to George B. Stewart, 16 May 1913, The Archives of the Burke Library (Columbia University Libraries) at Union Theological Seminary. New York, New York.

8. Henry Roe Cloud to Mary Roe, 11 April 1913, Roe Family Papers, Yale University Library, New Haven, Connecticut.

9. Henry Roe Cloud,"Education of the American Indian," *Report of the Thirty-second Annual Lake Mohonk Conference,* (Lake Mohonk Conference, 1914), 240–245.

10. Phil Zuckerman, *The Social Theory of W.E.B. DuBois* (Thousand Oakes: Pine Forge Press, 2004), 185.

11. John Dewey, *A Common Faith,* (New Haven: Yale University Press, 1960), 3.

12. Henry Roe Cloud to Progressive Education Association, 15 November 1928, Records of the American Indian Institute, 1908–1954, PCUSA Board of National Missions, West Lafayette.

13. Fayette Avery McKenzie, "The Assimiliation of the American Indian," *The Quarterly Journal of the Society of American Indians*, 1914: 137.

14. "History Making News." *The Quarterly Journal of the Society of American Indians*, 1914: 233.

15. Jon L.Brudvig, *First Person Accounts as written by American Indian Students.* 1996. http://www.twofrog.com/hamptonstories1.html (accessed July 22, 2009).

16. Arthur Parker, "The Awakened American Indian," *The Quarterly Journal of the Society of American Indians*, 1914: 269–274.

17. Mario R.Dinunzio, *Woodrow Wilson: Essential Writings and Speeches of the Scholar President,* (New York: NYU Press, 2006), 360.

18. Arthur Parker, "The Awakened American Indian," *The Quarterly Journal of the Society of American Indians*, 1914: 269–274.

19. "Wichita To Get Indian School." *The Wichita Eagle.* December 27, 1914: 1.

20. Ibid.

21. Ibid.

22. "A New Feather," *The Wichita Eagle,* 29 December 1914.

23. Henry Roe Cloud to Dr. H.B. Frissell, 31 January 1914, Records of the American Indian Institute, 1908–1954, PCUSA Board of National Missions, West Lafayette.

24. Henry Roe Cloud to E.E. Olcott, 27 October 1923, Records of the American Indian Institute, 1908–1954, PCUSA Board of National Missions, West Lafayette.

25. "Report of Henry Roe Cloud," Records of the American Indian Institute, 1908–1954, PCUSA Board of National Missions, West Lafayette.

26. Henry Roe Cloud to E.E. Olcott, 28 October 1924, Records of the American Indian Institute, 1908–1954, PCUSA Board of National Missions, West Lafayette.

27. "Roe Indian Institute," *The Southern Workman*, Press of Hampton Normal and Agricultural Institute,1917): 8.

28. Estimate of Administrative and Maintenance Expense for the School Year, 1916–1917, Records of the American Indian Institute, 1908–1954, PCUSA Board of National Missions, West Lafayette.

29. E.E. Olcott to Henry Roe Cloud, 13 January 1923, Records of the American Indian Institute, 1908–1954, PCUSA Board of National Missions, West Lafayette.

30. "A Challenge to Christian Indians," Records of the American Indian Institute, 1908–1954, PCUSA Board of National Missions, West Lafayette.

31. Henry Roe Cloud to E.E. Olcott, 3 April 1923, Records of the American Indian Institute, 1908–1954, PCUSA Board of National Missions, West Lafayette.

32. Henry Roe Cloud to E.E. Olcott, 9 May 1923, Records of the American Indian Institute, 1908–1954, PCUSA Board of National Missions, West Lafayette.

33. E.E. Olcott to Henry Roe Cloud, 31 January 1924, Records of the American Indian Institute, 1908–1954, PCUSA Board of National Missions, West Lafayette.

34. Henry Roe Cloud to Thomas Jesse Jones, 18 September 1923, Records of the American Indian Institute, 1908–1954, PCUSA Board of National Missions, West Lafayette.

35. Henry Roe Cloud to E.E. Olcott, 14 December 1923, Records of the American Indian Institute, 1908–1954, PCUSA Board of National Missions, West Lafayette.

36. E.E. Olcott to Henry Roe Cloud, 3 October 1925, Records of the American Indian Institute, 1908–1954, PCUSA Board of National Missions, West Lafayette.

37. W.B. Hill to Henry Roe Cloud, 6 January 1926, Records of the American Indian Institute, 1908–1954, PCUSA Board of National Missions, West Lafayette.

38. Edna R. Voss to Henry Roe Cloud, 22 March 1927, Records of the American Indian Institute, 1908–1954, PCUSA Board of National Missions, West Lafayette

39. Anna M. Scott to Henry Roe Cloud, 27 October 1927, Records of the American Indian Institute, 1908–1954, PCUSA Board of National Missions, West Lafayette.

40. Florence Goddard to Henry Roe Cloud, 28 February 1928, Records of the American Indian Institute, 1908–1954, PCUSA Board of National Missions, West Lafayette.

41. Florence Goddard to Henry Roe Cloud, 7 March 1928, Records of the American Indian Institute, 1908–1954, PCUSA Board of National Missions, West Lafayette.

42. Edna R. Voss to Henry Roe Cloud, 8 August 1928, Records of the American Indian Institute, 1908–1954, PCUSA Board of National Missions, West Lafayette.

43. Elsie Cook to Henry Roe Cloud, 12 December 1929, Records of the American Indian Institute, 1908–1954, PCUSA Board of National Missions, West Lafayette

44. Edna R. Voss to Henry Roe Cloud, 2 May 1932, Records of the American Indian Institute, 1908–1954, PCUSA Board of National Missions, West Lafayette.

45. Elizabeth Bender Cloud to Mary Roe, 26 January 1927, Records of the American Indian Institute, 1908–1954, PCUSA Board of National Missions, West Lafayette

46. Elizabeth Bender Cloud to Mary Roe, 10 November 1923, Records of the American Indian Institute, 1908–1954, PCUSA Board of National Missions, West Lafayette.

47. State of Kansas High School Principal's Report, Records of the American Indian Institute, 1908–1954, PCUSA Board of National Missions, West Lafayette.

Chapter Fourteen

Sleeping with the Enemy

Henry officially started working for the federal government in September, 1931. His efforts with the Institute no doubt contributed his appointment. So did his story. A Yale-educated Indian would provide positive public relations at a time when scarcely anything else seemed to be going well. Henry's work on the Meriam Report in 1928 elevated his status even more. The report, which was officially entitled *The Problem of Indian Administration*,[1] was commissioned by the Rockefeller Foundation and the Institute for Government Research. Henry was one of nine experts who were supervised by Lewis Meriam and charged with the responsibility of researching conditions about education, economics, health, the condition of women, living conditions, and discontent among the Indians. Others who contributed to the report were Ray A. Brown, Edward Everett Dale, Emma Duke, Herbert R. Edwards, the ever present Fayette Avery McKenzie, Mary Louise Mark, W. Carson Ryan, Jr., and William J. Spillman. William F. Willoughby, the Director of Institute for Government Research, submitted the report to Hubert Work, the Secretary of the Interior, on February 21, 1928. The report, in essence, stated the federal government's policies had been largely responsible for the impoverished conditions of the Indians. In addition to calling for a total overall of the government's policies, the report said that the goal of assimilation be abandoned. Control of education and most other functions should be transferred to the community level. When Henry began his work with the federal government, even though it had an inauspicious beginning, he had established a legacy with the Meriam Report.

Henry's primary role with the government was that of a traveling investigator, and his work frequently involved things other than education. He found his way to major Indian reservations like Pine Ridge and Rosebud in the North to the Choctaw Reservation in the South. He spent most of his time on the road and lived in hotels. His family continued to reside in Omaha. By this time Henry and Elizabeth had four daughters. Elizabeth Marion was born in 1917; Anne Woesha was born the next year; Lillian Alberta was born in 1920; and Ramona Clark was born in 1922. Their youngest child, Henry Roe Cloud, II., was born in 1926 but died three years later. Following a Winnebago tradition, the Clouds adopted the child of a family friend even though he, Jay Hunter, was not an orphan and raised him as their own.

In 1931 Henry testified before the U.S. Senate Subcommittee on Indian Affairs which was investigating the condition of Indians in the United States. His testimony dealt mostly with the issues of allotments and grazing on reservation land. While acknowledging that his recommendations were intended to provide the Indians with more autonomy and self-run, he also cautioned against blanket decisions or policies that did not take already existing and individual tribal conditions into account. His involvement with the subcommittee brought more attention to his experience and education.

One of Henry's more interesting investigations was that of the Haskell Institute in late 1932. Haskell was the crowning jewel of the government's Indian school system at that time. He found significant financial mismanagement centering primarily on the Athletic Association and the virtual control it had over the operation of the school. Haskell was operating an athletic program that had become nationwide in its involvement and appeal. Essentially it was taking the place of the Carlisle Institute in that regard, but Carlisle had been getting less competitive over the past decade. The success at Haskell came at a cost, and that cost was the effective and efficient administration of the school. Henry Cloud's report to the Indian Service included the surprising recommendation that Haskell revert to a vocationally oriented educational program and that the superintendent be an educator and not a politician or bureaucrat. He would shortly become even more involved in the affairs of Haskell. As President Hoover's administration came to a close and that of Franklin Roosevelt was about to begin, Henry's status was somewhat uncertain. In March of 1933 Henry was placed on administrative furlough. That period of unemployment did not last long. In May he was brought back to the Indian Service to serve as a field representative for the Indian Emergency Conservation Work program or the IECW. One of the alphabet soup programs of F.D.R.'s first hundred days, the IECW was the Indian equivalent of the CCC or Civilian Conservation Corp. He served in this capacity throughout the summer of 1933. He was then named, by Executive Order 6236, as the superintendent of Haskell Institute. This route was chosen to by-pass the sticky issue of the Civil Service exam. Once again Henry's life story served the government and himself well. *From Wigwam to Pulpit* was widely distributed.

Henry was thoroughly familiar with the situation at Haskell and knew that his job would be a challenge. The school was in debt, the problems were huge, and the school itself was enormous compared to the American Indian Institute. Henry's inability to deal in a timely with reports would not help either. The "red tape" of the Home Missions Board did not come close that of the federal government. He was also faced with having to deal with an Assistant Director of Education in the Indian Service who had been the assistant superintendent at Haskell, had served as acting superintendent, and who, more importantly, had wanted the position that Henry got. Henry had to report directly to Paul Fickinger, who went on to have a long career in the Indian Service and Bureau of Indian Affairs. Unlike at the AII, not everyone he had to deal with at Haskell wanted Henry to succeed. Chief among his opponents were the members of the Athletic Association. The whole situation was compounded by the fact that the newly appointed Commissioner of Indian Affairs, John Collier, demanded most of Henry's time to assist in the promotion of the Indian Reorganization Act. Much of the day-to-day administration at Haskell was left to the Assistant Superintendent, Robert Kelley.

In hearings before "A Special Committee on Un- American Activities in the House Of Representatives during the seventy-fifth Congress is 1939 testimony was given that stated "It was not long before Indians employed by the Commissioner were propagandizing for his program. Dr. Henry Roe Cloud, an ordained minister of the Presbyterian Church, a well-known educator, and a member of the Winnebago Tribe, was appointed superintendent of Haskell Institute for Indians. It can scarcely be said that Dr. Roe Cloud ever conducted Haskell Institute for during his entire time as superintendent until he was advanced to a position of supervisor of education at large in the Indian Bureau, he spent a great portion of his time visiting Indian reservations and exhorting them to accept the benefits of the so-called Wheeler-Howard Act."[2] While the witch hunt against John Collier and the B.I.A. was misguided, the assessment of Henry's time spent in his position at Haskell seems to be accurate. It is difficult to even say that at any time he was fully in charge. He was able to get the federal government to assume ownership of the stadium thus wiping out the school's debt. He instituted a policy of preferential hiring of Native Americans and encouraged the celebration and study of traditional Indian culture, festivals, and language. In his baccalaureate sermon entitled "Haskell and Her New Frontiers," he said that "Haskell Institute is definitely committed to the preservation of Indian race culture. We do not mean by this that Haskell Institute shall go forth and waste its energies in any petty attempt to preserve anything because it happens to be Indian. It recognizes on the other hand very clearly that there is in every race certain elements, practices and achievements extremely worthy of preservation, cultivation, and adoption."[3] However, there can be no doubt that John Collier thought that the passage and the implementation of the Indian Reorganization Act (the Wheeler-Howard Act) was his, and therefore Henry's, top priority.

John Collier was appointed Commissioner of Indian Affairs in 1933. He was described as being anything ranging from quirky to irritating. John was born in Atlanta, Georgia in 1884. His father, Charles Collier, was a prominent banker who was at one time mayor of Atlanta. John was educated at Columbia University and in France. He developed an intensive social awareness at an early age and worked with immigrants in New York. In 1919 he was appointed as the head of adult education in California. John's reform minded politics garnered the scrutiny of the Justice Department which was caught up in the Communist phobia of the time. Thinking it best to reduce his visibility, he moved to an artist colony near Taos, New Mexico at the invitation of artist Mable Dodge. It was there that he was introduced to Indian culture with the Pueblos. His scholarship, interest, involvement, and support never ended. In his 1938 report to the Secretary of the Interior, he said that "we took away their best land; broke treaties; promises; tossed them the most nearly worthless scraps of a continent that had once been wholly theirs. But we did not liquidate their spirit."[4] Upon his retirement in 1945, *Time* magazine called him, "the best friend the American Indian ever had."[5]

It is hardly surprising that the Indian Reorganization Act was called the Indian New Deal. The legislation was intended to reverse the long-standing policy of assimilation and to foster self-determination. The most controversial aspect of the IRA was to consolidate land that had been allocated to individuals through the Dawes Act and return it to tribal control. The lumber interest and ranchers who had leased much of this land were vehemently opposed. The reservations were empowered to adopt their own constitution if they so determined. Cloud was enlisted to help Collier explain the process and options to the Indians. Collier scheduled ten separate Indian congresses for that purpose, and Henry participated in half of them. He often assumed leadership in the question and answer portion of the meetings. There could be no question that he was there also because he was an Indian, and he was an Indian who had attended Yale, and was now a high ranking government official. His presence was to add credibility to not only the process but the IRA itself. He also met in smaller venues with Indian leaders to gain their support. He frequently invoked the much used road image by calling the IRA the "New Road." In 1936 Cloud's association, slight those it had been, with Haskell was ended. Commissioner Collier created the position of Supervisor of Indian Education for him. Despite the facts that he was only marginally responsible for supervising all of the educational work of the Indian Service and that the position sounded far more important than it was, his primary responsibility was to continue doing what he had been doing—trying to get the Indians to support the IRA.

Henry Cloud was clearly at the pinnacle of his career in government service in 1935–1936. He had worked tirelessly and effectively for the approval of the IRA and he had certainly received considerable attention in his position as Superintendent at Haskell, but his decline in prominence and influence occurred dramatically and precipitously. Forced by budgetary restraints, John Collier had to reassign several people in the Indian Service in 1939. Collier offered Cloud the superintendency of the Turtle Mountain reservation in North Dakota. This reservation was a relatively small one made up of remnants of different Chippewa Indian bands. Cloud rightfully saw this assignment as a demotion. It carried with it a smaller salary and a lower Civil Service rank. He also expressed a concern that the climate there might be harmful to his health since he had major reoccurring sinus problems. Collier, on the other hand, was adamant about making that particular assignment. Henry added another element to the argument by pointing out that the permanent position of Superintendent at Haskell had not been filled and that he would like to return. The Commissioner insisted that such a move was not going to happen and that Turtle Mountain was the only option on the table. This sparing continued and even intensified when Cloud more or less threatened Collier by saying that he was capable of proving that most of the Commissioner's program had been derived from a letter that he (Cloud) had sent him several years prior. Collier eventually modified his offer and told Cloud that he was going to be assigned to the Umatilla Reservation in Oregon—an even smaller reservation with an even greater pay cut.

It is difficult to determine why Cloud fell out of favor so quickly. His administrative ability, if measured by his willingness and ability to fill reports, etc. accurately, completely, and on time, was certainly lacking. He found himself on the wrong side of the political fence by declaring himself a Republican on several occasions in the middle of a Democratic administration. He was older; there were new Indians who were advancing in governmental service. Perhaps most importantly, he was no longer the public relations prize he once was. There were considerably fewer people who promoted him, supported him, and wanted him to succeed. Regardless, he took the job in Oregon and began his tenure as superintendent in 1939.

He was Superintendent of the Umatilla Reservation until 1948, and it was not an easy assignment. First, the reservation had been created for three tribes that had traditionally inhabited the Columbia Plateau region: the Cayuse, the Umatilla, and the Walla Walla. Second, the mere geography of the reservation complicated things. Parts of the reservation were arid and parts were extremely arable, but the overall landmass of the reservation had been substantially reduced over the years through the selling of allotments. The Reservation had rejected the IRA, and there was still a great deal of political squabbling and in-fighting. Part of the problem arose because of issues between "traditional" and "mixed bloods." The issue of fishing rights on the Columbia was also a complicated one. Fishing rights at Celilo Falls, which was located over eighty miles from the reservation were always problematic and involved negotiations with other tribes as well as the state. The federal government was building dams on the Columbia River, and while these construction projects did address current problems such as irrigation and future issues, such as hydroelectrical energy, they also affected the important salmon runs. Although Henry was well-known on the reservation because of his work in promoting the IRA and his appointment there was initially positively accepted, he did not have free reign or even an easy time as Superintendent. The tribe clearly was not just going to let him do whatever he wanted to. Ironically, Henry found himself in a position where he was receiving considerable criticism from several different quarters. A person who had once investigated and written about the problems with Indian administration now found himself part of the "problem." Exercising their local decision making authority, the tribe decided to hire its own attorney who would represent their interests, watch over their funds, and even investigate the superintendent. Henry was incensed and opposed the measure and the person designated to be the attorney. That person, Charles Luce, ultimately petitioned the Commissioner to remove Cloud from his position. In October of 1948 he was appointed Superintendent at the Grande Ronde-Siletz Agency on the Oregon coast. In December of that year, the agency was abolished. For the next two years Henry remained there to try to untangle complicated genealogical records to see who was entitled to portions of the 16 million dollars the government owed them.

NOTES

1. Lewis Meriam, *The Problem of Indian Administration,* Report of a Survey made at the request of Honorable Hubert Work, Secretary of the Interior, (Baltimore: Institute for Government Research, 1928).

2. *Investigation of Un-American Propaganda,* Hearings before a special committee, (Washington, D.C.: United States Government Printing Office, 1938), 2491.

3. Henry Roe Cloud, "Haskell and Her New Frontiers," *The Indian Leader,* (Haskell Institute, June 1932).

4. John Collier, *Annual Report of the Secretary of the Interior for the Fiscal Year Ended June 30, 1938,* Annual Report, Washington, D.C.: United States Government Printing Office, 1938.

5. "Indian Fighter,"*Time,* 19 February, 1945.

Chapter Fifteen

The End of the Chosen Road

Wo-Na-Xi-Lay-Hunka, Henry Clarence Cloud, Henry Roe Cloud, Dr. Henry Roe Cloud died on February 9, 1950. He suffered his second heart attack and died in his sleep. He was in Siletz, Oregon to address the Beach PTA. *The Indian Leader*, the Haskell Institute newspaper that had called Cloud "the foremost Indian educator" in America in 1935 simply reported the facts: "Dr. Henry Roe Cloud, superintendent at Haskell from 1933–1936 died in his sleep February 9 at Siletz, Ore., where he had been tracing family histories to determine eligibility of Oregon coastal Indians for a court award of 16 million dollars in payment of an early land seizure by the government."[1] *The New York Times* said that Cloud "typified those who break away from wigwam ways to the complexities of modern civilization."[2]

Some nine years before, Mary Roe had died as a result of an automobile accident on June 16, 1941. She had just left a meeting of the National Fellowship of Indian Workers that had been held in Farmington, New Mexico. She had lived to see the rise and decline of Henry Roe Cloud. Her undying belief that it was his destiny to lead "his people" never waned. Ironically, it was at a meeting of the National Fellowship, just a few years later, that Robert Chaat, a Comanche who had attended but did not graduate from the American Indian Institute and who had been ordained in 1934, talked about the presence of three roads that were open to Native Americans. He said that "the Indian Road was a good road in its time...but the old Indian way of life cannot meet the needs of today and a different generation, no more than a dirt road can meet the demands of modern traffic. The White Man's Road has contributed much to the spiritual welfare of the world and has done wonders in the development of the God-given resources of the earth (but this material wealth) has not helped the white man's road to be the Jesus Road."[3] Mary Roe's death, as much as his demotion, marked yet another turning point in Henry Cloud's life. His greatest promoter, advocate, and supporter, his "mother," was gone. A little over a year later Henry suffered his first heart attack. The Women's Board of Domestic Missions said of Mary, "At the meeting in Farmington, it seemed that her life work had received its crown of glory. All present eagerly sought her advice, and her long and rich experience impressed those present at the conference with a deep feeling of reverence. Her messages to them during the devotional hour will never be forgotten. They were like a valedictory."[4]

Fifteen years after the death of her husband, Elizabeth Bender Cloud died in 1965. She had been an active part of his work since their marriage and figured prominently into the work of the (Roe) American Indian Institute. When she spoke to the female students at Genoa School in 1917, her message was typical of her values and approach. She said that there is "nothing better than living a pure life, both in mind and body"[5] and that it was critically important to be kind to each other. Her combined messages about family values and Indian education vaulted her to national prominence when, after Henry's death in 1950, she was chosen National Mother of the Year by the American Mothers Committee. According to one newspaper, her message was of "patience, talent, love, and good citizenship."[6] Her dedication to education was shown in the fact that "one of their daughters went to Wellesley, two to Vassar, (and) one to Stanford."[7] In keeping with her father's pioneering example, daughter Elizabeth Marion was called the first Indian to graduate from Wellesley. She was an active member of the Grange, the National Conference of Social Workers, the National Conference of American Indians, and the Federation of Women's Clubs. She represented Clackamas County (Oregon) to the White House Conference on Children

NOTES

1. "Dr. Roe Cloud Dies," *The Indian Leader,* Haskell Institute, February 24, 1950).

2. "Dr. Roe Cloud, Indian Life Expert, Dies," *The New York Times,*
(The New York Times, 12 February 1950).

3. LeRoy Koopman, *Taking the Jesus Road,* (Cambridge: William B. Eerdman Publishing Company, 2005), 188.

4. "Tribute to Mrs. Walter C. Roe," *Intelligencer-Leader,* 19 September 1941: 22.

5. Virginia Barker, "Mrs. Roe-Cloud Talks to the Girls," *The Indian News,* (Genoa Indian School, 1917).

6. "First Mother," *The Oregon Journal,* (The Oregon Journal, 29 April 1950).

7. Ibid.

Chapter Sixteen

What If

Like everyone's life, Henry's was full of "what if's." What if his grandmother had said that she was just too busy or too tired to tell Henry stories in his youth? What if his uncle had not accepted his traditional role of teacher? What if, after the deaths of his parents and grandmother, he lapsed into deep depression and just gave up? What if William T. Findley had not made that late night call? What if he had "returned to the blanket?" What if Mount Hermon had proven not to be to his liking, and what if he simply grew tired of his constant money problems? What if he did not get into Yale? What is he did not happen to meet Mary Roe? What if the Roes just did not have the time or energy for another "project?" What if he had not listened to Walter Roe's advice about his future? What if the Roe Institute had succeeded? What if Franklin Roosevelt had not appointed John Collier Commissioner of Indian Affairs? What if Henry had stayed at Haskell Institute? The "what if" questions could obviously go on and on without answers, but there are others that exist that can be answered. Why did Henry fall from grace with Collier and the Indian Service? Why was he exiled in relatively insignificant posts for the rest of his life? Why did he even decide to start working for the federal government anyway? Why did he generally avoid mainstream politics and focus almost exclusively on Indian issues? What really was his legacy?

Even if we acknowledge that the conditions he experienced in his youth were in some ways problematic and perhaps even enough to classify him as "high risk" using today's vernacular, and I do not believe that he would have, Wo-Na-Xi-Lay-Hunka's evolution into Dr. Henry Roe Cloud really is not surprising. Emmy Werner and others have researched and written about resiliency for many years. Cloud had at least two things in his favor that mitigated factors that might have been overwhelmingly negative to others. His failure of the Civil Service exam notwithstanding, he had a keen intellect. More importantly, he knew the value and necessity of working hard. He knew that his early education did not put him on equal footing with other students at Mount Hermon and Yale. So, he realized that he had to work harder. Second, throughout his life, despite the frequent transitions, he had people, family, friends, and mentors who believed in him and supported him. People wanted Henry Roe Cloud to succeed, and he did.

At heart, Henry Roe Cloud was not an administrator or even really an educator. He was a missionary and an Indian leader very much in the image that Walter Roe had created for him. He had to know a lot about many things to be such a leader. He knew about land allotments; he knew about health problems and care; he knew about fundraising and public relations. He had to stay in contact with, and know, "his people," even if he did just call them "the Indians." Being known as, and in the position of, an educator gave him the credibility and the platform to address many different issues, problems, challenges, and possible solutions. Being an educator gave him an audience, and in many ways this was his real pulpit.

Cloud benefitted from being a curiosity, and he knew how to use that fact. He was recognized and well-known at Mount Hermon and Yale primarily because he was an Indian, but also because he made a conscious effort to do everything, join everything, play everything, and run for every office that he could. He knew that the distinction of being the first American Indian to graduate from Yale would serve him well later. In fact, the requests for him to speak, etc. came so frequently that he had long periods of absence from both Oberlin and Auburn and affected him academically. Clearly Cloud had established his priorities. He was never assigned to a church, but he entitled his autobiography "From Wigwam to Pulpit." He made addresses about the perspective of the anthropologist, but he received his Master's Degree in absentia from Yale after a program of guided readings rather that course work and a thesis. He embraced being a "Yale Man," and never discouraged use of the university's name in his introductions, but after he graduated he never seemed to be interested in returning. He did make visits to Mount Hermon, Santee and Genoa. Ironically, one of Yale's secret societies, Skull and Bones, is presently being sued by the great-grandson of Geronimo who claims that members of the society robbed his great-grandfather's grave in 1918 and stole his skull. A recently discovered letter seems to support that claim. In some respects Cloud was an Indian curiosity—just like Geronimo. Cloud was an investigator who reviewed numerous issues on many different reservations, schools, etc. He was observant, and his reports were detailed and very readable. Unfortunately, they were also almost always very late. He seemed to make career decisions that resulted in replacing one level of bureaucracy and administrivia with another more complex one, and he had difficulty handling them at all levels. Henry Roe Cloud was many things, and that was the problem. He was too many things.

What Henry Cloud could do was to talk. He could talk equally effectively with Indians and with whites. He was also able to get those people to talk to each other. He could bridge cultural and linguistic gaps perhaps better than anyone else of his time. He never forgot what it was like to be unable to talk with his father in his native language after attending the government school. I disagree with what the *New York Times* said about his typifying "those who break away from wigwam ways to the complexities of modern civilization."[1] He stood well-grounded, but with one foot squarely in each culture. He was active in Pan-Indianism. The only real Indian traditions that he rejected outright were the traditional religions with what he called their paganism and the newer Native American religions with their peyote use. Even in this he was more moderate or ambivalent than most.

If Wo-Na-Xi-Lay-Hunka had been born fifty years later, he probably would have been a statesman or an elected official. He had that kind of presence. However, because his career ended inauspiciously when it did, few people know his name today. The first assumption when Henry Roe Cloud's name is mentioned is that there is some connection to Chief Red Cloud. Despite that fact, he was one of the few Native Americans who was represented on a float in President Johnson's 1964 inaugural parade.

He was present and involved in most of the important events of the time that concerned Native Americans. He met with Presidents, Secretaries of the Interior, Commissioners of Indian Affairs, philanthropists, and millionaires with one agenda—improving the conditions for American Indians. Unfortunately, his efforts, like most of those involving the original Americans resulted in promises and programs that were broken, short lived, or which never lived at all. Now, over half a century after his death, allotment and trust issues still exist, the Bureau of Indian Affairs is still a lightning rod for criticism, traditional and "new Indians" are still at odds, and there is still disagreement about teaching native languages and culture. Perhaps the most important question about Henry Roe Cloud that has emerged through this and other investigations is simply, what would things for Native Americans be like today if it was not for people like him?

NOTE

1. "Dr. Roe Cloud, Indian Life Expert, Dies," *The New York Times,* (The New York Times, 12 February 1950).

Bibliography

Adams, David Wallace. *Education for Extinction.* Lawrence: University Press of Kansas, 1995.

Alumni Association of Yale. *The Songs.* http://alumninet.yale.edu/classes/yc1961/songs.htm (accessed July 14, 2009).

Arthur C. Parker, editor. *The Quarterly Journal of the Society of the American Indian,* 1916: 15.

Barker, Virginia. "Mrs. Roe-Cloud Talks to the Girls." *The Indian News.* Genoa Indian School, 1917.

Bear, Luther Standing. *Land of the Spotted Eagle.* Lincoln: University of Nebraska Press, 1978.

Brudvig, Jon L. *First Person Accounts as Written by American Indian Students.* 1996. http://www.twofrog.com/hamptonstories1.html (accessed July 22 2009).

Cajete, Gregory. *Look to the Mountain: An Ecology of Indigenous Education.* Durango: Kivaki Press, 1994.

Camp, Lewis Sheldon Welch and Walter. *Yale: Her Campus, Class-rooms, and Athletics.* Boston: L.C. Page and Company, 1899.

Carol Barrett, editor. *American Indian Biographies, Revised Edition.* Pasadena: Salem Press, 2005.

"Catalogue." *Catalogue of Mount Hermon School.* Mount Hermon: Press of E.L. Hildreth and Co., 1898.

Catalogue of the Oberlin Theological Seminary: 1910—1911. Oberlin: Oberlin College, 1911.

Clark, Rev. Francis Edward. *The Christian Endeavor Manual.* Boston: United Society of Christian Endeavor, 1903.

Cloud, Henry. "Henry Cloud and Tennent Church." *The Word Carrier.* Santee: Santee Normal Training School, May—June 1905.

Cloud, Henry. "Mission to the American Indians." *the Yale Courant,* 1909: 520—523.

Cloud, Henry Roe. "An Antropologist's View of Reservation LIfe." *Northwest, Inter-mountain, and Montana Superiontendent's Conference*. Pendleton, September 11, 1941.

———. "An Appeal to Christian People." Lake Mohonk, October 19, 1910.

———. "Education of the American Indian." Lake Mohonk, 1914.

———. "Education of the American Indian." *Report of the Thirty-second Annual Lake Mohonk Conference*. Lake Mohonk: Lake Mohonk Conference, 1914. 240—245.

Cloud, Henry Roe. "In Memoriam: Alfred Longley Riggs." *The American Indian Magazine*, 1916: 180—183.

———. "From Wigwam to Pulpit." *Missionary Review of the World*, May 1915: 400—413.

———. "The Winnebago Medicine Lodge." *The Christian Intelligencer*, December 22, 1909: 833.

———. "The Indian's Relation to the Community." *The Twenty-Eighth Annual Lake Mohonk Conference*. Lake Mohonk: Lake Mohonk Conference, 1910. 14—16.

Collier, John. *Annual Report of the Secretary of the Interior for the Fiscal Year Ended June 30, 1938*. Annual Report, Washington, D.C.: United States Government Printing Office, 1938.

Crum, Steven J. "Henry Roe Cloud: A Winnebago Indian Reformer; His Quest for American Indian Higher Education." *Kansas History*, 1988: 171—184.

Cynkar, Robert J. "Buck v. Bell: "Felt Necessities v. Fundamental Values?" *Columbia Law Review*, 1981: 1418—1461.

Daddario, Wilma A. "They Get Milk Practically Every Day." *Nebraska History*, 1992: 2—11.

Deloria, Ella. *Speaking of Indians*. Lincoln: University of Nebraska Press, 1998.

Dewey, John. *A Common Faith*. New Haven: Yale University Press, 1960.

Dinunzio, Mario R. *Woodrow Wilson: Essential Writings and Speeches of the Scholar President*. New York: NYU Press, 2006.

Donald Warren, editor. *American Teachers: Histories of a Profession at Work*. New York: Macmillan Publishing Company, 1989.

"Dr. Roe Cloud Dies." *The Indian Leader*. Lawrence: Haskell Institute, February 24, 1950.

"Dr. Roe Cloud, Indian Life Expert, Dies." *The New York Times*. New York: The New York Times, February 12, 1950.

Eastman, Charles Alexander. *From Deep Woods to Civilization*. Mineola: Dover Publications, Inc, 2003.

———. *From the Deep Woods to Civilization*. Mineloa: Dover Publications, 2003.

Edwin Rogers Embree, editor. *Life at Yale*. New Haven: Yale University Press, 1912.

Elihu Society. http://www.elihu.org/ (accessed July 14 , 2009).

Fetter, Frank. "Imperialism and Cosmopolitanism." In *The Cosmopolitan Annual*. Ithica: Cornell University, 1907.

Findlay, James. "Education and Church Controversy: The Later Career of Dwight L. Moody." *The New England Quarterly, Vol. 39, No. 2*, June 1966: 210—232.

"First Mother." *The Oregon Journal*. Portland: The Oregon journal, April 29, 1950.

Flower, J. Cecil. "The Religion of the Peyote Cult of the Winnebago Indians." In *Approach to the Pyschology of Religion*, by J. Cecil Flower, 58—116. Whitefish: Kessinger Publishing, 1927.

"Haskell and Her New Frontiers." *The Indian Leader.* Lawrence: Haskell Institute, June 1932.

"History Making News." *The Quarterly Journal of the Society of American Indians*, 1914: 233.

Hoxie, Frederick. *Talking Back to Civilization" Indian Voices from the Progressive Era.* New York: Bedford/St. Martin's, 2001.

Intelligencer-Leader. "Tribute to Mrs. Walter C. Roe." September 19, 1941: 22.

Investigation of Un-American Propaganda. Hearings before a special committee, Washington, D.C.: United States Government Printing OPffice, 1938.

James T. Brown, editor. *Catalogue of Beta Theta Pi.* New York: James T. Brown, 1917.

Koopman, LeRoy. *Taking the Jesus Road.* Cambridge: William B. Eerdman Publishing Company, 2005.

Lewis, Bonnie Sue. *Creating Christian Indians.* Norman: University of Oklahoma Press, 2003.

Maragret L. Archuleta, Brenda J. Childs, Tsianina Lomawaima, editors. *Awawy from Home: American Indian Boarding School Experiences.* Phoenix: Heard Museum, 2000.

Meriam, Lewis. *The Problem of Indian Administration.* Report of a Survey made at the request of Honorable Hubert Work, Secretary of the Interior, Baltimore: Institute for Government research, 1928.

"Mount Hermon." *Record of Christian Work*, 1905: 246.

"New Yale Senior Club." *New York Times.* New York: New York Times, March 21, 1903.

North, Woesha Cloud. *Informal Education in Winnebago Tribal Society with Implications for Formal Education.* Lincoln: The University of Nebraska, 1978.

Nuwer, Hank. *Wrongs of Passage: Fraternities, Sororities, Hazing, and Binge Drinking.* Bloomington: University of Indiana Press, 2002.

Page, Elizabeth M. *In Camp and Tepee.* New York: Fleming H. Revell Company, 1915.

Parker, Arthur. "The Awakened American Indian." *The Quarterly Journal of the Society of American Indians*, 1914: 269—274.

Radin, Paul. *The Autobiography of a Winnebago Indian.* New York: Dover Publications, 1963.

———. *The Trickster: A Study in American Indian Mythology.* New York: Schocken Books, 1956.

———. *The Winnebago Tribe.* Lincoln: University of Nebraska Press, 1990.

Ramierz, Laura M. *Keepers of the Children: Native American Wisdom and Parenting.* Reno: Walk in Peace Productions, 2004.

"Regarding the Indian School." *The Pipe of Peace.* Genoa: Genoa Indian School, July 31, 1891.

"Remarks." *Report of the Thirty-fourth Annual Lake Mohonk Conference.* Lake Mohonk: The Lake Mohonk Conference, 1916. 53-54.

"Report of the Executive Council." *First Annual Meeting.* Washington, D.C.: Society of American Indians, 1912. 7.

"Roe Indian Institute." *the Southern Workman*, 1917: 8.

Rose, William J. "Remarks of Nehwarts." *Proceedings of the Twenty-second Annual Meeting.* Lake Mohonk: The Lake Mohonk Conference, 1904. 56.

Saleeby, Caleb Wiiliams. *Parenthood and Race Culture: An Outline of Eugenics. .* New York: Moffat, Yard, and Company, 1909.

"Santee Normal Training School." *the Word Carrier.* Santee, Nebraska, November 1900.

Smiles, Samuel. *Self Help.* New York: American Book Company, 1904.

Sorci, Thomas. "Latter Day Father of the Indian Nations." *The News*, Summer 1988: 17—19.

Stockel, H. Henrietta. *Shame and Endurance.* Tucson: The University of Arizona Press, 2004.

Symmes, Frank R. *The History of the Old Tennent Church.* Cranbury: George W. Burroughs, 1904.

Tetzloff, Jason M. *To Do Some Good Among the Indians: Henry Roe Cloud and Twentieth Century Native American Advocacy.* West Lafayette, IN: Perdue University, 1996.

"The President's Visit to Mount Hermon." *The Hermonite.* Mount Hermon: Mount Hermon School, September 20, 1902.

The Wichita Eagle. "Wichita To Get Indian School." December 27, 1914: 1.

Thomas, Grace Powers. *Where to Educate: A Guide to the Best Private Schools, Higher Institutions, etc. in the United States.* Boston: Brown and Company Publishers, 1898.

Time. "Indian Fighter." February 19, 1945.

Tripp, Bessie. "Bessie Tripp's Letter." *The Pipe of Peace.* Genoa, Nebraska, May 16 Friday, 1891.

W.B. Backus, Superintendent. "Third Annual Report." *The Pipe of Peace.* Genoa, Nebraska, August Friday, 1891.

Wegner, Tisa. *We Have a Religion: The 1920s Pueblo Indian Dance Controversy and American Religious Freedom .* Chapel Hill: The University of North Carolina Press, 2009.

Wilkins, David Eugene. *American Indian Politics and the American Political System.* Lanham: Rowan & Littlefield Publishers, 2006.

Woodruff, C.D. "Tomah Indian school." *The Milwaukee Sentinel.* Milwaukee, July 22, 1894.

Woods, Frank. "Second Session." *Proceedings of the 13th Annual Lake Mohonk Conference of Friends of the Indians.* Lake Mohonk: The Lake Mohonk Conference, 1896. 104.

Woonspe-Wankantu. Santee, Nebraska: Santee Normal Training School Press, 1901.

Zuckerman, Phil. *The Social Theory of W.E.B. DuBois.* Thousand Oakes: Pine Forge Press, 2004.

Index

alcohol, 52, 75, 79–80
American Indian Institute, x, 98–99, 103–6, 104n12, 107n47, 109, 113–14
"An Anthropologist View of Reservation Life," 6
appendicitis, 68
Arapaho, 46, 77
assimilation, 11, 15–16, 25, 32, 92, 107, 110
Auburn Theological Seminary, x, 81–82, 116

Backus, W.B., 10–11, 13, 14n6, 14n9
Band of Mercy, 17
Battle Ground Farm, 35–36
Bender, Elizabeth, 93–94, 101–2, 106nn45–46, 114
Bender, Charles Albert, 93
Beta Theta Pi, 41, 43n4
blindness, 47, 72, 94
Board of Trustees, (American Indian Institute), 97–100
boarding school, 9, 15–16, 19, 20, 30
Borden, William, 89
Brainerd, David, 35–37, 53
brains and efficiency, 95
Brown, James T., 43n4
Bureau of Indian Affairs, x, 109, 117

Carlisle Indian School, 10–11, 48, 73, 94, 103, 108
Celilo Falls, 112
Chaat, Robert, 113
"A Challenge to Christian America," 108
Chase, Hiram, 94
Cheyennes, 13, 46–47
Chiricahua Apache, 62, 84
Christian education, 28, 88, 91, 97
Christian Endeavor Society and Manual, 76, 79, 81, 110
Christian Indians, 8n12, 42, 47–49, 105
Civil Service, 101, 108, 111, 116
Cloud, Henry Roe, *Also* Henry Clarence Cloud: at Auburn, 82–87; childhood and early life, 1, 2; conversion at Winnebago Reservation School, 15–19; death, 113; demotion, 111; Genoa School experience, 14; at Mt. Hermon, 27–37; at Oberlin, 75–81; *The Problem of Indian Administration,* x, 92, 107; Principal of Roe (American) Indian Institute, 87–106; name changes, 14, 49; relationship with Mary Roe, 49–51, 62, 67–68; relationship with Walter Roe, 49– 51, 116; role in Society of

American Indians, 92–94; Santee Indian School experience, 20–23; Superintendent at Haskell, 109–11; traveling investigator, 92–94; at Yale, 39–69
Cloud II, Henry, 108
Cloud, Lillian Alberta, 108
Cloud, Ramona Clark, 108
Collier, John, 109–12, 112n4, 115
Colony, Oklahoma, 46–48, 60, 65–66, 79, 84, 95, 102
Commissioner of Indian Affairs, 12, 25, 80, 95, 101, 109–12, 115, 117
Committee of One Hundred, 99
Cosmopolitan Club, 42, 43n10, 71
Creek Indian, 56
Cross Day, 16–17
Crum, Steven, ix, xin3
Cruz, Juan, 80
Cutler, Henry F., 28–29, 32, 34, 35, 37nn7–9, 38n10, 38n18, 38nn20–21

Dabb, Edith, 60
Daughters of the American Revolution, 98
Dawes Act, 110
day schools, 15, 20
Dewey, John, 21, 91, 104n11
Dodge, Dora, 34, 38n18
Doxon, Charles, 78
drunkenness, 46, 49, 51
DuBois, W.E.B., 73, 91, 97, 104n10
Dutch Reformed Church, 100

Earthmaker, 4–5, 48
Eastman, Charles, 20, 23n4, 28, 33, 37, 37n6, 42, 66, 77, 80
educational philosophy, 37, 81
Elihu, 41, 43n7, 50, 57, 58, 64, 66, 89
eugenics, 85, 86n7
Executive Order 6236, 108

fasting, 2, 4, 6–7, 36, 48
Fickinger, Paul, 109

Findley, William T., 16–19, 29, 48–49, 54, 115
fishing rights, 112
flag pole hill, 51
fraternity, 41–42, 50
From the Deep Woods to Civilization, 23n4, 37n6
From Wigwam to Pulpit, 17n1, 7n3, 8n8, 8n17, 14n3, 14n7, 19n3, 19n5, 23n6, 23n9, 34, 37, 38n22, 39, 41, 43n1, 55n9, 88, 104nn4–5, 108, 116
fundraising, 97–98, 100–101, 103, 116

Garvie, James W., 22
George Junior Republic School, 87, 90
Geronimo, 62, 116–17
Goddard, Florence, 100, 105nn40–41
Golden Rule Circle, 13
Good Feather Woman, 1
Good Government Club, 33
Grande Ronde-Siletz Agency, 112
Genoa Indian School, x, 7, 9–14, 14nn4–6, 14nn8–9, 16, 19, 22, 30, 89, 114, 114n5, 116
government schools, ix, 14, 16, 29, 32, 40, 94, 103, 108
Grant Institute, 10, 11, 13, 14n4. *See also* Genoa Indian School

Hampton Institute, 57, 79, 93–94, 97, 104n15, 105n27
Hard to See, 1
Haskell Institute, x, 96, 108–9, 111, 112n3, 113, 114n1, 115
Hensley, Albert, 48, 51–52
Hill School, 45, 62
Hill, William Bancroff, 89, 98–100, 105n37
Hoare, Lucie, 102
hok-i-ku, 2
Home Missions Board, 101, 109
House Un-American Activities Committee, 109, 112n2

Index

Hunter, Jay, 108
Hyde, A.A., 97

Indian agent, 15, 46, 53, 79
Indian Emergency Conservation Work, 108
Indian New Deal, 110
Indian Quarterly, 92
Indian Reorganization Act, 109–10
Indian reservations, 44, 107, 109
Indian schools, 13, 20–21, 92–93,103
Indian Service, 108–11, 115
Indian Territory, 10, 45–46, 48, 52, 80
Institute for Government Research, 107, 112n1
Interior Department, 95, 99, 107, 110, 112n1, 112n4, 117
International Red Cross, 24

Jesus Road, 47, 55n2, 56, 69n15, 113, 114n3
Jicarilla Apache, 61
Johnson, William E. "Pussyfoot," 80

Keller, Albert G., 84–85, 86nn9–10
Keller, Helen, 72
Kelley, Robert, 109
King's Daughters, 13

Lake Mohonk Conference, 2, 7n4, 8n19, 34, 38n19, 44–45, 49, 55n11, 60, 69n10, 78, 82, 87, 90, 94, 97, 104n2, 104n9
Lane Rebels, 75
Lewis, Bonnie Sue, 4, 8n12
Life at Yale, 42, 43n9
Lindquist, G.E.E., 101, 102

manu-mental education, 20
McKenzie, F.A., 76, 92–94, 104n13, 107
measles, 12
Medicine Lodge, 4–5, 8n14, 19n4, 41, 48, 51–52, 54, 73

Meigs, John, 62, 64
Meigs, Marion Butler, 62, 63, 64
Meriam Report, x, 92, 107, 112n1. See also *The Problem of Indian Administration*
mescal, 48–49, 51–52
missionaries, 9, 36, 46–47, 50–51, 53–54, 56, 61
Moffett, Thomas C., 87
Moody, Dwight L., 27–29, 33, 37n5
Mount Hermon, x, 23, 27–30, 32–33, 35–37, 38nn10–18, 38nn20–21, 71, 79, 81, 97, 115–16

Nahwats, 49
National Conference of American Indians, 114
National Fellowship of Indian Workers, 113
native languages/tongues, 11, 13–14, 21, 47, 117
New York Times, 41, 43n8, 113, 114n2, 117, 118n1
North, Anne Woesha Cloud, 1, 8n5, 108
Nunn, "Honest John," 18

Oberlin Theological Seminary, x, 75–76, 79–81, 81n1, 82–83, 116
Ohiyesa, 20–21. See also Eastman, Charles
Olcott, Eben E., 88, 97–99, 104n24, 105n26, 105n29, 105nn31–33, 105nn35–36
Old Tennent Church, 35–38, 38n24
one-eyed reservation, 94
Onondaga Indian Reservation, 82

Page, Elizabeth, 4–5, 8n11, 8n13, 44, 47, 55n1, 55nn4–5, 55n7, 55n12, 55n16, 62, 68, 70n31
Pan-Indian organization, 77, 80, 117
Parker, Arthur, 81n7, 95, 104n16, 104n18
Pawnee, 9–10, 98–99
Periconic, 49

Peace Club, 95
peyote, 48–49, 51–52, 78, 117
Phelps-Stokes Fund, ix, 92, 98
Phi Beta Kappa, 50, 58, 89
Pipe of Peace, 10–11, 13, 14nn4–6, 14nn8–9
pogroms, 71–72
"powder keg of Europe," 24
Pratt, Richard Henry, 11, 103
Presbyterian Church, 16, 20, 37, 45, 63, 82–84, 88, 100, 109
The Problem of Indian Administration, 107, 112n1. See also Meriam Report
Progressive Education, 21, 92, 104n12

Radin, Paul, 2–4, 8n7, 8nn9–10
Railroads, growth of, 25
Rave, John, 48
reservation school, 15–16, 22, 29–30
Riggs, Alfred L., 5, 21–22, 23n5, 29, 37n9, 48, 97
Roe Indian Institute, x, 41, 89–90, 97, 99, 105n27. See also American Indian Institute
Roe, Mary Wickham, x, 42, 44–51, 56–68, 77, 79–81, 89, 93–94, 98–99, 113–14
Roe, Walter, x, 5, 42, 44–51, 56–68, 81, 83–84, 87–88, 90–91, 94, 96, 115–16
Roosevelt, Franklin, 108, 115
Roosevelt, Theodore, 33–34

Scott, General Hugh, 99
secret societies, 41–42, 66
Sells, Cato, 95
Smiles, Samuel, 22, 23n8
Santee Normal Training School, x, 19–23, 23nn1–2, 29–30, 34, 36, 37n7, 37n9, 38n23, 38n25, 60, 89, 96, 116
Smiley, Albert, 44
social gospel, 75–76, 80
Society of American Indians (SAI), 76–77, 81n4, 92–94, 104nn13–14, 104n16, 104n18
The Soul of the Indian, 80
storytelling, 2–3

Stewart, George B., 83, 85nn2–3, 88, 104n7
Sorci, Thomas, ix, xin2, 38n26
The Southern Workman, 85, 97, 105n27
Stewart, Philo, 75
Stokes, Anson Phelps, 88
Student Volunteer Movement, 68

Taft, Jr., Robert A., 40
Tomah Indian School, 15, 19n2
Trachoma, 94
Trickster, 3–4, 8n9
Thorpe, Jim, 73
Tuberculosis, 13, 36, 45
Tubman, Harriet, 82–83
Tulley, Dawn, 102

Umatilla Reservation, 111
Union Theological Seminary, 83, 85nn2–3, 104n7, 104

Voss, Edna R., 100, 105n38, 105n42, 105n44

war clan, 2
war clubs, 95
Wheeler-Howard Act, 109–10. See also Indian Reorganization Act
"White Man's Burden," 25
White man's road, 113
White Earth Reservation, 93
Wilson, Woodrow, 93–95, 104n17
The Wichita Eagle, 96, 104n19, 104n22
Wichita, Kansas, 41, 96–98
Winnebago culture and traditions, x, 2–7, 7n7, 7n10, 7n14, 13, 14, 108
Winnebago people, ix, 1–4, 7, 13, 16, 18, 19, 19n419, 21, 30, 38, 40, 48–49, 51–52, 64–65, 69, 73, 75
Winnebago Reservation, 1, 15, 21, 40, 49–52, 64–65, 69, 73, 75, 79, 82, 89, 93, 96
Wo-Na-Xi-Lay-Hunka, 2–7, 9–14, 23, 25, 56–57, 64, 73, 103, 113, 115, 117

The Word Carrier, 20, 23n2, 36, 38n23, 38n25
Wright, Frank Hall, 45–46, 51, 72

The Yale Courant, 52, 55n19
Yale University, x, 4, 36–37, 39–42, 43nn2–3, 43n9, 47, 49–50, 53–54, 56–57, 62, 67, 73, 81, 83–85, 86n6, 87, 89, 104n11, 107, 110, 115–16
Young Men's Christian Association (Y.M.C.A.), 33, 42, 47, 57, 65, 68, 87–89, 96
Young Women's Christian Association (Y.W.C.A.), 60, 87